Traveler

OTHER WORKS BY PHILLIP BERRY

Stones Across the River

Every Day is Game Day

Traveler

A Poetic Journey

Phillip Berry

Copyright © 2021 by Phillip Berry

Published in the United States by Cross Stone Press.

All rights reserved. No part of this book may be reproduced or transmitted in any form or by any means, electronic or mechanical, including photocopying, recording, or by any information storage and retrieval system, except in the case of brief quotations embodied in critical articles and reviews, without prior written permission of the publisher.

Although the author and publisher have made every effort to ensure the accuracy and completeness of information contained in this book, we assume no responsibility for errors, inaccuracies, omissions, or any inconsistency herein.

If you would like to do any of the above, please seek permission first by contacting the author at www.phillipberry.com.

Printed in the United States of America

ISBN Hardcover: 978-0-9981689-5-1
ISBN Paperback: 978-0-9981689-6-8

Editor: Madison Choiniere
Cover and Interior Design: Ghislain Viau
Cover Art: *Washington Street* by Erin Spencer
Author Photo: Jessica Bishop

For Cooper, Reagan, and Fulton.
May you always see God in the beauty, innocence,
and truth of the poetry all around you.

Contents

Foreword — xv

Introduction — 1

Stumbling Forward 2005 – 2008 — 5
- Wholeheartedly (01.22.05) — 6
- Stillness Lies Within (06.02.05) — 8
- Split Second (10.10.05) — 9
- Quietly (12.27.05) — 10
- His Grace (12.27.05) — 11
- Dragonfly Thoughts (01.10.06) — 12
- Quiet Directions (01.21.06) — 14
- Chameleon (01.25.06) — 16
- Witness (1.30.06) — 18
- More (02.13.06) — 20
- Playing the Part (02.22.06) — 21
- This Heart Grasps (04.1.06) — 23
- How Will You Remember Me? (05.08.06) — 25
- Hint (07.13.06) — 27
- Destiny (07.13.06) — 29
- Intended (07.17.06) — 31

Selflessly (07.22.06)	33
Waters (07.22.06)	35
Restless Horizon (08.23.06)	37
Strangely Fulfilled (09.4.06)	39
The Silent Room (09.4.06)	41
Beyond Me (09.25.06)	42
I'm Not Finished (09.25.06)	44
With the Rain (09.27.06)	45
Watching You Grow (11.05.06)	47
In My Words (11.13.06)	49
Sleep Alone (11.13.06)	51
Lights of Christmas (12.10.06)	52
For Madison (12.10.06)	54
His Purpose (01.29.07)	56
On Madison's Birthday (04.10.07)	58
In the Dark (07.02.07)	60
With Kellen at Deep Creek Lake (07.08.07)	62
Hungry (07.08.07)	63
Watching You (07.08.07)	64
Morning Angels (07.09.07)	65
Imagine (11.29.07)	67
Relationships (01.27.08)	69
You Came Home *for Kiefer* (03.23.08)	71
Have Faith (09.29.08)	73
Grandma Huff (09.30.08)	76

To His Purpose (10.12.08)	78
In Your Space (10.12.08)	80
Steps Toward Conversion 2009 – 2016	83
Forty (02.11.09)	85
First Steps (09.02.09)	87
Unready (09.02.09)	89
Fleeting Essence (09.04.09)	90
You Stood There (09.05.09)	91
No Longer There (09.05.09)	92
More Remains (09.05.09)	93
Gone (09.05.09)	94
For Madison *at Roy's Passing* (09.07.09)	95
Play it Again (09.11.09)	96
I See You There (07.01.10)	98
Greatest Strength (09.11.09)	100
Shadows of Summer (09.14.09)	102
Looking for Contemplation (01.28.10)	103
The Span of Time (07.01.10)	105
With Macy (01.11.11)	107
John D. (03.12.11)	109
Time Well Spent (08.24.11)	111
These Days (08.30.12)	112
Northwind (08.08.14)	114
Loud with Memories (12.10.14)	116

Still the Same (04.04.15)	118
Surrender to Complexity (04.04.15)	120
I Weep *at Ben's passing* (04.29.15)	122
Do Your Best (05.27.15)	123
If Only (05.27.15)	125
Of Our Own Making (05.27.15)	127
Shared on a Summer's Eve (06.10.15)	129
Your Words (07.03.15)	131
Liberty (07.03.15)	132
Uncertain (07.12.15)	134
Gone (08.06.15)	136
Vulnerable (09.06.15)	140
Imperfect (12.19.15)	142
Sharing Silver (25 years together) (12.22.15)	144
Spent (06.09.16)	147
Macy (07.04.16)	148
Forgive me Grandma (07.04.16)	150
The Afternoon (07.06.16)	152
Words Unread (07.09.16)	153
Shift (08.04.16)	155
Emma Stone (08.04.16)	157
I'm Sorry (pictures on the piano) (08.04.16)	159
Lost in a Shifting Shadow (08.07.16)	161
Passing (08.07.16)	163
Joy (08.07.16)	165

Beyond (09.05.16)	167
Remembering (09.11.16)	169
Fall's Leaves (11.01.16)	173
Called to More (11.01.16)	175
Your Greatest Gift (11.01.16)	177
Seasons of Life (11.26.16)	179
The Moments Before (12.24.16)	181
The End is Near (12.24.16)	183
I See You *for Baby Choiniere* (12.24.16)	185
Walking with Conviction 2017-2020	**187**
Not so Bold (01.10.17)	189
In the Beginning (01.14.17)	191
The Way of a Pilgrim (01.24.17)	194
Your Best Work, Your Peak Years (01.29.17)	196
That Moment (02.26.17)	198
Possibility (04.23.17)	200
In the Dark (04.29.17)	202
When the Lights Go Out (05.04.17)	204
Dreaming of Bernadette (06.03.17)	206
The Old Nemesis (06.09.17)	208
Cooper (06.24.17)	211
Life of Opportunity (07.01.17)	213
Sowing (07.15.17)	214
Inscrutable Purpose (08.26.17)	215

I Choose Faith (09.14.17)	217
As You Leave (11.13.17)	220
Smiling, I Close My Eyes (01.07.18)	222
Beacon (01.07.18)	224
The Difference (01.07.18)	225
The Here and There of the Unseen (01.13.18)	226
Twelve Months (02.10.18)	229
Growing into You (02.15.18)	231
Evening Sun (02.25.18)	233
Scars (03.05.18)	234
Falling Days (05.11.18)	236
The Choice (06.06.18)	238
The Truth (06.10.18)	240
Shreds (06.12.18)	242
Reunion (06.12.18)	244
Why? (07.10.18)	246
I Walk On (07.15.18)	248
Faith (08.02.18)	249
Each Step (08.03.18)	250
The Evening Calls (08.24.18)	251
Remembering (09.03.18)	253
News (09.24.18)	255
Changes (11.03.18)	258
Gratitude (11.22.18)	260
January Spring (01.08.19)	261

Enough (01.28.19)	262
The Book of Eli (05.12.19)	264
Intersection (05.12.19)	265
Reflection (06.30.19)	266
Reagan (06.30.19)	268
Dawn (08.06.19)	270
The Things We Found (11.11.19)	272
Santiago (11.12.19)	274
Pilgrim (11.12.19)	276
Finisterre (11.13.19)	279
The Way (11.23.19)	281
The Next Step (01.09.20)	283
Walking Away (02.13.20)	284
Steady (03.24.20)	285
One *for Reagan* (05.23.20)	287
Toward a Waiting Tomorrow (11.25.20)	288
JMJ for Fulton (03.28.21)	290
Traveler (04.12.21)	292
About the Author	295

Foreword

Phillip Berry brings hope to the restless and weary traveler in us all through these beautifully crafted poems.

By entering into his personal journey, we find companionship and courage, joy and sorrow, and the strength to face life's defining moments head on.

No matter where you find yourself on your own journey, Traveler will not only inspire you to carry on faithfully, but to stop and enjoy the view along the way.

Though our destination may feel distant, we know we are headed somewhere beautiful and that we are not alone.

Let your heart find rest in this raw and poetic portrayal of a man who has faithfully walked the path laid before him and come to know something greater than himself.

Madison Berry Choiniere

Introduction

I was once asked: "What kind of book will you write next?" "It will be a book of poetry," I replied. She answered, "Oh, I don't really care for poetry." I smiled as I told her, "That's ok, most people don't."

Knowing that most people don't care for poetry, why would anyone create a book of it? I have long felt called to pull this book together. It isn't the result of an intentional act of "writing a book" but the gathering of poems capturing particular moments spanning fifteen years of my own life. As I began to compile this book, I realized that the poems within it reflect a window of time and tell a story. It's all in here: loss, struggle, doubt, fear, and uncertainty as well as victory, exuberance, joy, hope, determination, and clarity. This book is a collection of pieces that stand individually

Traveler

---

as well as collectively, painting broadly and narrowly within one span of one life. However, they also cast a reflection of the world in a series of words that challenge and encourage, ultimately serving hope to those willing to see it.

Why write a book of poetry? Because.

One reason many dislike poetry is because they do not understand it or know how to read it. I am no expert on poetic style and this book is not compiled for the expert. This book is for the curious, those wondering, those seeking, and those asking. You see, the best way to read these poems is through your own lens. The titles, the words, the phrases, the stories, and any clear meanings should evoke your own experience. They should speak to you where you are and within the context of your own life. The best poetry becomes the possession of its reader and is effective to the extent that it is made relevant in the reading. If one word, phrase, passage, or poem strikes you in a particular way, that is a measure of success. If the body of the work takes you somewhere else within your own existence, along your own journey, then count it as a wonderful accomplishment. I certainly will.

I did nothing to link the poems, edit them toward one another, or attempt to rework them to my current state of mind. Some of them are quite raw, reflecting the rawness of a moment. My intention is that any who delve into this

Introduction

book will find comfort and discomfort in equal measures. My hope is that the challenge of finding a particular poem's cadence or interpreting a specific line will attract rather than discourage. Ultimately, the work should help you see your story in a different way and the journey of it should help bring that story into focus. In the process, you'll get glimpses of the author and perhaps feel no less about your own story in his failings of craft, logic, or artistry.

The title, "Traveler," reflects our place on life's journey. Moving about on the highways and byways of our existence, we experience time's passing and the world's wonders like tourists who visit a while before returning home. Along the way, we see interesting destinations, but the collective passing through is what makes them truly intriguing. Good and bad, we move through experience, becoming that next version of ourselves; this is the part that is so incredibly fascinating. We are all travelers.

The cover painting by Erin Spencer depicts the mundane scene of a westward drive along Washington Street in Indianapolis but in such colorful fashion that it brightly evokes a sense of possibility in the travel along life's roads. Each is a doorway to adventure and growth. As I write this, the physical place depicted in her work is very much a part of my journey and apropos to the notion of traveling the roads through the moments of our lives.

Traveler

The simple everydayness of the view makes it poetic and magical for me.

   Phillip Berry

Stumbling Forward
2005 – 2008

Wholeheartedly (01.22.05)

There is so little
To which I give myself
Wholeheartedly
My life a collection
Of half-heartedness
I wake with feelings
Of grand possibility
Only to lose each notion
Amid the shattered rocks
Of my own distractions
"Action is the enemy of thought"
And I've watched the movements
Slay intentions mercilessly
My own hand left holding the blade
The will within seems a pitcher
Bent on pouring itself
Into every intricate cup
Alas its contents remain frozen
No little part of which
Flows into any corner of my day
Distraction moves the moments
And therein drains

Stumbling Forward 2005 – 2008

The morning's ambition
Leaving me tired and frustrated
One more time
Let me pour myself
Into just one ambition
And release the fire
Of singular wholeheartedness
Freeing my own elemental intent,
Putting to wing this phoenix
From my ashes

Stillness Lies Within (06.02.05)

Quietly
I slip to that sanctuary
Between the noise of reality
And unconsciousness
For long have I been absent
Unable to find still waters
My heart beats calmly
No longer agitated by uncertainty
I feel more control
By letting go

Stumbling Forward 2005 – 2008

Split Second (10.10.05)

The morning air broken
By the siren's cry
The haunting tones,
At once urgent and mournful,
Echo through the streets
Pleading for attention
Announcing sadness

Perhaps an unknown life
Has been altered
Unexpectedly visited by fate
These movements in destiny
Surround us
Yet we barely notice

The sounds fade
The birds continue
Their twitchy search for food
The waiter returns with coffee
Life goes on

Quietly (12.27.05)

The world comes
Quietly
Passing me in the night
Each moment
A recollection
Of all that's lost
Unable to hold them
I cry
Quietly
Wishing those snapshots
Would stop
Suspended before me
Open to view
Always at a leisure
I don't have
The tiptoe movement
Of a fragile life
Escapes me
Quietly

Stumbling Forward 2005 – 2008

His Grace (12.27.05)

Digging within
Watching without
Moving in small ways
Enveloped in doubt

Lessons bequeath
Their humbling touch
While lying beneath
Hope, fear and such

It isn't a game
Though the score seems unfair
The limp and the lame
Left with never a care

Struggling on
In destiny's command
Hope all but gone
We glimpse His fair land

Beckoned, we stumble
Toward God's soft embrace
Life's left us humble
Prepared for His Grace

Dragonfly Thoughts (01.10.06)

Dragonfly thoughts
Haunt my mind
My focus flitting across
This expanse of distractions
The night's restlessness
Grips me
Moving my listlessness
Attentively
The walls reflect
Some deep boredom
Disinterest my quiet companion
I suspect fatigue
The culprit in this affair
My body rebelling
Against a heightened alert
Poised to strike
Hourly throughout my day
Even the numbness
Promised by the television
Does little to soften
The buzzing in my ears
Now agitated past fatigue,

Stumbling Forward 2005 – 2008

Perhaps respite awaits
In the haven
Of your deep brown eyes

Quiet Directions (01.21.06)

The words read
Like today's news
As real and immediate
As the day they were written
The nights have passed
Quickly
Leaving that traveler
Far behind
Only my recollection
Holds those realities

The mysteries
Still haunt me
The answers
Remain elusive
But the desperate urgency
Has faded
Replaced with a patient longing
To continue the journey
The frantic days
Still come
While the dreams remain
Stoic against the world

Stumbling Forward 2005 – 2008

Traveling back
I found paths
Trodden
By circular wandering
Those dark forests
Were smaller than remembered
The open sky
Always closer
Than I knew
It seems easier
Though questions remain
Giving them to Him
A new possibility
The cathartic answer
To all that lies
Beyond me

Hold this patience
The fire still burns
Below. Within. Around.
Let it hold you
Calmly caressing
Your impulsive nature
Until Wisdom whispers
Quiet directions

Chameleon (01.25.06)

The day's light
Reveals nothing of my colors
This form taking shape
Only against a solid context
Moving between
The textures
Of buildings and furniture
I morph fluidly
Adopting the look
The dimension
The façade of my surroundings
These days I wonder
Of my true form
The effortless shedding
Of these skins
Hides the churning sense
Of responsibility within
Offers an unseen comfort
Fluid motion in this
In-between existence
No time for boredom
Each second is precious

Stumbling Forward 2005 – 2008

In the fragile balance
The words move
In an environmental litany
Dictated by a supernatural
professionalism
My life a perpetual commercial
For the goods, services, hopes
Of my entrepreneurial masters
Yet, the chameleon remains
Unchained.
Free to move within
And beyond the walls
Of commercialism
The changing sheens
Become shallow surface coat
To the complexities
Shadowed beyond the colors
Flexible, malleable
Impenetrable
Reality remains closed
Held by the chameleon

Witness (1.30.06)

As I bear witness
To the fluid world
Around me
I hear the voice
Of the spectator
Mixing words of hope
Despair
Joy and outrage

Life mirrors the game
Our movements reflect our being
On and off the court
Character is tempered
In the heat
Of the game
The higher the stakes
The sharper the edge

My steel remains
Malleable
Still soft from
My own fires
Those edges forming

Stumbling Forward 2005 – 2008

Against the pressures of experience,
The struggles,
And the doubts

The forge consumes me
Molding my form into the oneness
Now defining me
Witness to the day
And all her reminders
I rest comfortably
Among a thousand
Sharpened spears

The day remains incomplete
Managed by necessity,
The directionless hope
Of my own naiveté
Experience carves
the paths of wisdom
but there are places remembered,
witnesses to my memory

More (02.13.06)

Into the quiet
I walked.
Split within
I waited.
Is that the hand of God
Upon my brow?
Hoping for some purpose
Revealed in pictures
I can see.
Wanting desperately
To understand His meaning,
We give ourselves to the unknown,
Daily.
Unknowingly casting our lot
Among the broken shards
Of noble intentions.
Forgetting our own failings
Before the reflections of hope.
Resting silently upon our eyes.
Reaching always for something more,
Even while it all lays at our feet.

Stumbling Forward 2005 – 2008

Playing the Part (02.22.06)

The days come quickly
Moments of clarity in tow
Darting in between,
We feel the building pressure
Of futures unknown

The fragile nature
Of what we hold
Lies forgotten
Amid the numbing
Flash of the urgent

Blissfully unaware,
We charge headfirst
Into unknown possibilities
With only blind faith
To reassure our steps

Blessed are we
To hold such strength
Blind though it may be
Real power lies in belief
This place seems its last bastion

Traveler

Hope remains with belief in purpose
The mysteries enfold
Our small actions,
Comforting the tender wounds
Of time's battles

When you feel the only piece left to hold,
Perhaps then you are ready.
Embrace that which is yours
And take your place on His stage,
Playing the part,
for which you were meant

Stumbling Forward 2005 – 2008

This Heart Grasps (04.1.06)

The moment is here
But the words remain aloof
Evasive, they float out of reach
The night moves slowly on
Then springing forward
Still, the quiet is restless

Agitated, this heart grasps
Reaching for the solace
The words provide
The need goes unanswered
Defied by the dark's
Unresponsive nature

The frustration
Lays palpable on still lips
Consuming
The evening reprieve
Masking the shadows
With a silent anger

Directionless
Inert
History's lens

Traveler

Appears so clear
Casting light on former unknowns
Leaving the obvious

The present remains obscured
Drowned in point-of-view
Context remains relative
To the truths it reveals
While fact falls dead
Under the glare of the camera

Reality seems a difficult thing
The lens always distorting
Even shared events vary
From one party to the next
Changing with time
And her distorting impositions

Reason falls under human view
Twisted to purposes
As varied as those
Whose intentions mold the story
The incontrovertible heaving-to
As this heart grasps

Stumbling Forward 2005 – 2008

How Will You Remember Me? (05.08.06)

How will you remember me?
Impatience and intensity
Wound up
Into extreme expectations?

Will it be the quiet moments?
Bedtime and car rides,
Tenderness in the stillness
After the pains

The malcontent
Dissatisfied with today,
Always yearning for the future
Possibility of things to be

Or the believer?
Endless cheerleader
Wanting success for you
In whatever you chose

The yeller or the singer?
The games we played,
Or the endless corrections,
As I tried to lead you into maturity

Traveler

Will you remember my mistakes
Or the times I succeeded?
Will my example inspire your greatness
Or warn of places to avoid?

Is it my love you'll carry
Or my failings as a father?
The sum total of my inadequacies
Easy to behold

Through it all,
I only want for you to hold
A living sense
Of my undying love

Stumbling Forward 2005 – 2008

Hint (07.13.06)

One hint
The smallest indicator
And my heart soars
Hope remains powerful
The tiniest spark
My world looks different

The days feel repressive
I've forgotten my own fire
No longer believing, unable to see the light within
Acknowledged by one stranger
I feel different, validation in some fashion
Igniting the flame of hope

As life is fragile
The shadow of hope
Remains even more delicate
Crushed under the slightest pressure
But it takes time to convince us
That we aren't worthy

Tonight I'll sleep with a smile
Dreaming in memory
Floating among the strength

Traveler

Hiding in recollection
God's gift is to remember
My responsibility remains

Stumbling Forward 2005 – 2008

Destiny (07.13.06)

I never believed in the fantasy of destiny
Self-made and self-reliant,
I carved my own way
Through life's adversities

Along the way,
I was humbled
Laid low by the world
Self-reliance, a dream I once had

Now I see purpose in roads walked
Reacting to a higher power
It's time to relinquish a control
I never had

With hope I see a path,
A way through the obstacles
No self-creation, but a gift
Part of some larger plan

This hope I'll embrace
Though it may pass
The days will move
Each piece to its place

Traveler

Letting go can be difficult
Giving of myself
In order to let it happen
The difficult lesson of adversity

Good will overcome,
As evasive purpose
Reveals itself at the appointed time
Witness it, then let it happen

Intended (07.17.06)

The moments pass
Promising nothing
Leaving traces across
All of my hidden desires
Offering no release
To those aspirations
Life is a marvel
Giving and taking
In unequal amounts
The spectrum of emotion
Lies beyond comprehension
The joy and sorrow
Consumes us all
It is with trepidation
That I face my days
Walking unknown paths
My character is tested
Though I can see no purpose
I hold to the notion
Like a raft in angry waters
The answers must lie ahead
The passion will come

Traveler

These days move on
And my memory fades
Till only a shadow remains
Have I forgotten how to live?
Did I ever know?
I hate myself for asking
It feels like weakness
The wonder brings confusion
Showing up every day
Waiting for a sign
My lines all but forgotten
In this ongoing drama
I know You're there
Watching, waiting
For me to wake up
Into the man You intended

Selflessly (07.22.06)

In the light
Of the fading day
Mysteries reveal
Their hidden purpose
The shadows release
Forgotten hopes
Giving them to the sky
In cloudy pantomime

The dusk holds
Life's movements
In her silent aspect
Hinting at closures
For which we search
Like some ancient map
The falling radiance
Draws us into ourselves
Opening our hearts
To wordless revelations

In the end it is our own silence
That hides purpose
Locked within our souls

Traveler

Rests the story of our life
Clarity comes by letting go
Of tomorrow
And embracing today
Not in physical abandon
But the soft embrace
Of a fragile loved one
A tender acceptance
For the sake of acceptance
Wanting nothing more
Than a safe moment
Expecting nothing in return

Accepting today
Selflessly
Opens the gate
To your destiny

Waters (07.22.06)

The water fell
Systematically
Patterned in the mechanics
Of modern irrigation
Spraying liquid life
Onto thirsty foliage

I wondered about our thirsts
The cravings for quenching
Wants, needs, passions
Our days sprinkled
With life-giving moments
Feeding those places hidden
And revealed

In each turn of the sprinkler
I fell to another place
At once present
And walking in the past
In holding the moment
History seemed to embrace me
Holding me up as if baptized
In some water of life

Traveler

All those moments
Led to this place, this person
The currents molding, guiding
Forcing an evolution
All to arrive now
Exactly as intended
Precisely timed
Depths I cannot understand
Nor is it for me to know

The waters circling
One last time
Till the quenching is done
I'm left with the rhythm
Echoing in my mind
Holding cravings
I'm happy to release

Stumbling Forward 2005 – 2008

Restless Horizon (08.23.06)

Fatigue
    Consumes me
Days of frantic endeavor
    Culminating in exhaustion
Complete in its depletion
    Of my last reserve

Emerging from these ashes
    A dormant restlessness takes me
Resurrecting feelings
    Long forgotten
Restoring desires
    From their quiet slumber

On this edge
    I can feel the weight
The overwhelming presence
    Of impatient ambition
Those old expectations
    Gnawing at my sense of peace

The angst brings push-pull emotions
    To sharpen my senses

Traveler

For an acceptance
    I cannot handle
Driving me with thoughts
    I can't abide

Let sleep take me
    Smother the noise
Restore my soul in
    Night's blackness
Tame the restless giants
    Of this gypsy spirit

Strangely Fulfilled (09.4.06)

Fall comes near
The season of renewal
The shortening days
Call for something different

The quiet murmur
Of this restless heart speaks
Forcefully demanding
A shift with the days

The moon moves
Towards fullness
Reminding me
Of forgotten strengths

A silent promise haunts my dreams
In words I can't discern
The world seems close
Set on an edge to be revealed

I walk blindly on
Along known paths
Into the unfamiliar
There is no hint of what awaits

Traveler

And I feel
Strangely fulfilled
By notions of thoughts unknown
and words yet to be said

The Silent Room (09.4.06)

In the night
Silence can overwhelm
A nervous energy
Vibrating the air

The quiet reveals
The disquiet underneath
Uneasy noisiness
Permeating the room

The house creaks
While crickets call
But the silence is far louder
Announcing a disconnect

Peace is not here
The day has left
Unfinished business
Things undone

The churning echoes
In my head
Stirring me
Into restlessness

Beyond Me (09.25.06)

The days darken
With winter's approach
The turning leaves
Portend a change
As I feel myself
Turning with this season

Autumn's restlessness
Seems infectious
Yet I suspect
That my own inclinations
Equal any tumult
Nature turns my way

Invisible currents
Electrify the air
While crisp days
Hold the visible
Streams of clouds
Like some avian migration

Blue skies with
An impossible clarity
Draw my eye to a bright vastness

Stumbling Forward 2005 – 2008

Within which I can lose direction
My senses reeling
From a sense of the impossible

Improbable witness I remain
As the marching endlessness of time
Stains my memory
And the moments slip through
Desperate fingers
As I grasp at my own inadequacy

This life is beyond comprehension,
A faltering one-step-at-a-time existence
My only claim to some sense of control
The illusion complete,
As I convince myself
That I have a voice in my own destiny

I'm Not Finished (09.25.06)

Let me think
More of myself
A higher opinion
Of someone I no longer believe in

When did I last think
That anything was possible?
The sadness of a lost friend grips me
Where are you, Possibility?

Bring the light of aspiration back
Touch me with wonder
So that my eyes will water
With the joy of the unknown

Experience conspires
To rob my youth
Take the freedom of desire
Waste the reckless abandon of fearlessness

Give it back
I'm not finished

With the Rain (09.27.06)

The rain falls
Pouring small drops
Like salvation
Over the visible world
The steady rhythm,
A soothing baptism,
Chasing anguish away

Cool air escorts the dampness
Completing the moment
With the comfort of moist breaths
An irregular patter of errant drops
Accents the ensemble
While intermittent thunder
Punctuates the scene

The world seems to sigh, enfolded
In the private experience the storm brings
Sharing its gifts
While retreating to a sacred sanctuary
Remembering similar moments,
Walking along recollection
Amidst the weather

Traveler

With the rain falls another element,
The invisible currents of inner stillness
Our own waters placid and serene
We glide toward an infinite horizon
Hope and expectation coupled
With a secret knowledge of more
There is more to come

Stumbling Forward 2005 – 2008

Watching You Grow (11.05.06)

Watching you grow
I see my own moments,
Lost in time
Days of discovery
And possibility

Watching you grow
I recall the times of my life
Victories and failures
Dotting the landscape
Of my existence

Watching you grow
I realize that the best is before us
Opportunities of life waiting to be seized
Through you I'm reminded: it's a story just started
And each day leaves another line

Your victories and failures
Are yours, not mine
The life you're building, yours to direct
I am the spectator, cheering, cajoling,
Pushing you toward all you can be

Traveler

Watching you grow
My life has new meaning,
Purpose beyond myself
I'll share your life, while I can
Then let you embrace, all that it might be

Watching you grow
I love life more,
See it more clearly,
And relish the gift
Of watching you grow.

Stumbling Forward 2005 – 2008

In My Words (11.13.06)

Looking at my words
I feel sadness and exhilaration
This path seems littered
With anguished musings
Of hope and longing
While I'm inspired
By my own craft
In capturing the moments
Each line takes me
To a singular emotion
Frozen to a memory
My essence plucked from time
In the grip of my words
It is a gift
If only for my self
To hold timelessly
Each precious thought
Filled with the texture of emotion
Remembered in these pages
The words an index
To the greater story
A written key

Traveler

To the untold stories
Of my life
Grace blesses me
Enables me to stop here
Amid these memories
Suspended between the words
Of a riddle known to me

Sleep Alone (11.13.06)

You leave me
    To the silence of the night
The cold bed beckons
    Calling me to solitude

Your voice echoes
    Wordlessly
Never leaving me
    Though you've gone

In the colors, the movement
    Of this room
I see you
    Feel you upon me

Small symbols
    Grace the night
Announcing your connection
    To these moments

You are not here
    But I feel you
As I lift the blankets
    To sleep alone

Lights of Christmas (12.10.06)

As the lights shimmer
I'm taken to other days
Celebrations that had no meaning
Beyond their own festivity

Years later
I slowly grasp
These lights and
Their implication

My children wander
The days of cheer
Anticipating, participating
In all our Catholic traditions

But I know the
Thinking will grow
To something more
With time

There is a Holiness
In this season
This pause to breath-in
Life that's granted and to celebrate

Stumbling Forward 2005 – 2008

My children grasp more
Than I know
While I'm still grasping
Growing along a slower path

I pray that the lights
And wreaths and trees
Always hold the deeper meaning
For the faithless among us

May I forever grasp
The human ties in this
Divine, Holy Day
And the impact of the season

Let them twinkle,
These lights of Christmas
So we never forget
And move memory to action

For Madison (12.10.06)

A year ago
You gave this journal to me
Inviting me to travel its pages
With my words
I embrace the opportunity
With a tender touch
Hoping to never lose
These moments you've offered
The months pass
As you change before me
Growing into the person of God's will
You are strong & courageous
Inspiring and empathetic
Capturing a bit of you here
Seems the ideal use of my pages
In those soft blue eyes
Sparkles a possibility
An endless glow
Hungry for the world
There is nothing you can't do
Nowhere you can't go
If you choose

Stumbling Forward 2005 – 2008

Blessed to be in
Your orbit
I hold these days
Possessively
Time wrestles me
As I fight to hold on
Knowing it all must move
In its own direction
A tinge of sadness
Trembles along my pen
But I find myself thankful
For your brightness in my life
However long I'm gifted
With its warmth

His Purpose (01.29.07)

The sunrise gripped me
Bathing me in recollection
Moments long forgotten
Illuminated in the pink and purple sky
Clouds accented the moment
Framing my vision
In the unreality of this time
Why is it so easy to forget
The long roads and many faces
Which brought me here?
Voices returned, captured
In the silent break of day
And with them came possibility
Chasing my darkest moments
With a silvery edge
Now with closed eyes
I can find that path
The glow guiding me
To places within, behind
Doors left closed
It seems I've cast so much aside
Haphazardly

Stumbling Forward 2005 – 2008

Oblivious to the randomness
Never intending to return
But return I must
Like the farmer to his field
I've come to harvest
My forgotten yield
The days quicken
With the realization of purpose
Hope commands my attention
Stillness has returned
With an energy
Your time is now
Seize the day!
Remember times past
The many-faced loves
Of your life
Passions left incomplete
Demand closure
This moment, this day
You will move forward
Opening those doors
Remembering and creating
Fulfilling His purpose for you

On Madison's Birthday (04.10.07)

Thirteen years
I've watched you grow
The long path
Has been so brief
We've shared defining moments
As you've become the young lady
Before me
I see your face
Change before me
The baby's features melt away
And the little girl emerges
Bold and active
You sprinted from the gate
Always caring
You sought to please
And you still do
It's been my honor
To share your triumphs
On the court, in the field
You've been a force
Our special moments
Sharing thoughts

Stumbling Forward 2005 – 2008

I've grown with you
I always wanted to be like you
I feel that sadness
Looming at the thought
Of you growing up
But it is only joy
Holding me
Pride in who you are
And the person yet to be
I've shared myself
All that I am
In hope
That you'd be more
Knowing all the while
That you already were
My inspiration, my angel
My hero
On this 13th birthday
This pivotal moment
Of moving towards your future
I hold you close
Thanking God for the chance
To have you in my life

In the Dark (07.02.07)

My days pass
In quiet agony
I struggle to find meaning
In these moments
The now seems
More elusive than ever
As I watch my children
Slip into the future
While time fades into the past

The sense of something more nags me
A purpose beyond understanding and grasp
Lies in the fringes of perception
Are these daily struggles the sum of my existence?
My energies flung in all directions
Where should I focus?
Attainment seems like some obscure end
No particular desires to move me
No ambitions to drive me forward

I lay awake, saddened by unrecognized sensation
An angst over some missed opportunity
My accomplishments seem hollow

Stumbling Forward 2005 – 2008

An empty collection of activities
Adding to little, barely memorable
Is melancholy merely a bad attitude?
The joy seems barren
I tell myself "things are great"
But I remain unconvinced

The night's dark energy
Grips my soul in its cold embrace
Tendrils piercing waning hope
With sharp antagonism
The rally will come
Strength will return,
But for now, tearless
I let the last remnants of this day
Leave me, drained and lonely

With Kellen at Deep Creek Lake (07.08.07)

The morning sun reveals
This great expanse
Whose heart it steals
With breaking wave
And soft breeze
My heart I gave
Under these green leaves

Your little voice
Bright with hope
Gave me little choice
Held me, like rope
As I listened with smile
You went on and on
Limitless imagination
Mile upon mile

Your endless possibility
Heartens me
With joy and curiosity
You see only good
And adventure at each turn
Reminding me when I could
Perhaps, I still can learn

Hungry (07.08.07)

Lapping at the shore
Hungry and happy
The lake wanted more
But could the land give enough,
So that they both might live?

Watching You (07.08.07)

Bright day, warm breeze
The air holds promise
Birds sing in the trees

You walk along tied boats
Imagining battles
Amid towers and moats

Watching you
Unfettered imagination

Fantasy and illusion
You have all that you need
To fly off
Away to distant places

Sometimes
In my better moments
I let you take me too

Stumbling Forward 2005 – 2008

Morning Angels (07.09.07)

The breaking sun
Uncovers the waiting world
A slowly moving day
Moves up on the slumbering
I watch it happen
As though it's the first
Two visions approach
Golden halo'd
Blue and brown eyes
Greet me – my morning angels
"Certainly" is all I can muster
To respond to the request
Bright smiles entrance me
As I watch them
Inspirations to my life
I see the purpose I need
In their being
These blessings I don't deserve
But it is my greatest
Proof of God
Gifts so wonderful
Cannot be random

Traveler

These purposeful creations
Brighten the universe
Making all the difference

Imagine (11.29.07)

The night grows quiet
With the slowing of my heart
Like retreating footsteps
The beats soften
I've been waiting for this moment
World melting away
Leaving impatient stillness

Hopes and regrets surround
As I embrace the night
Wrapped in its solace
I find clarity between emotions
Though logic falls short
My innocent faith
Fuels reluctant comfort

Stepping away from the incessant debate
Burdening these days,
Doubt inflicting paralysis
Becomes easy to see
I reach for the calm
An understanding of my own powers
And the Presence that gifted them

Traveler

Undeserving, unsure, weak
The clear air reveals
Each blessing,
Every possibility
There is still time, He whispers
Promising a destiny
I've yet to imagine

Stumbling Forward 2005 – 2008

Relationships (01.27.08)

I read once
That relationships
Define a good life
The connection to others
Defines our legacy
Touchpoints on the journey
Defining the flavor
Of the memories we leave
No obituary will capture
Our lasting impact
Or fill any empty hole we leave
Life seems to spare
Little space for friendship
Nagging demands,
Artificial priorities
And the daily sense
Of a race to the finish
Leave other connections
Laying cold on the ground
Where did we lose the need for others?
Of course, we didn't,
It lies there, on the table

Traveler

Covered by the remote, the bills,
The thousand shallow imposters

Stumbling Forward 2005 – 2008

You Came Home *for Kiefer* (03.23.08)

You came back to me
Clearly affected by time and distance
The longing for home
Was on your face
Longing for you, on mine

Your collection of experiences
Rolling off your tongue
I listened: of pubs and parades and people
You embraced a broader world
Then let it embrace you

Is it possible that leaving me
Helped you step toward your self?
The self-discovery of independence
And pressing that self against the world
Those edges help us see ours

I revel in the brightness
Your eyes convey pure, boyish, enthusiasm
Though you rest on the edge of manhood
The simple joy of a gift
And pleasure of returning

Traveler

I suppose it's another edge of fatherhood
Letting go as you step forward
Each day moving toward a place
That is yours alone

But today, you are mine
For a moment more,
You are mine

Have Faith (09.29.08)

I listen
While talking heads
Cackle sound-bite observations
Bereft of depth or meaning
Verbal bombs, designed
Not for enlightenment,
But for attention.
The magnetic blast
Of sensationalism

For weeks they've gone on,
Spitting platitudes
About this, our most important election
Dissecting candidates
With attempts at insight
While the machines grind on
Churning America in the slow rising
Temperatures of socialism

Now it's fear
On the verge of collapse
Our economy teeters
In the hands of the politicians

Traveler

Ripe with the stench
Of opportunism
The heads banter on
All-but-saying how stupid we are
For not getting it
For not giving in

How far we've come
From the small republic built
On democracy
Now the loudest voices and biggest contributors
Rule our land
Perhaps it's not so different
But it feels ominous

It's far from over
The voices of cooler heads emerge
There are alternatives
And maybe the sun will rise again tomorrow
I'm left with resentment
A seething anger for a machine
I can't see
Frustration with mouthpieces
Spouting fear

Stumbling Forward 2005 – 2008

Though my soul is troubled
I defy their message
Refusing to succumb
To hopelessness

Faith holds me
A belief in possibility
And a nation of believers
The ideals fought for
And paid in blood
The mindless chatter fades
Before the quiet night
They are not the doers
The builders of our nation
Only the takers
Living on the backs
Of the strong

My heart calms
The voices fade
God's touch is upon us
Our mission incomplete
Have faith
Have faith

Grandma Huff (09.30.08)

You passed quietly
No drama or fight
The call came early
Leaving me to ponder this new world

Though not my blood
I've grown up with you there
My life with Sally
Accented by your presence

There are no words
For the expected
No solace for the inevitable
The grief must run its course

The funeral followed your plan
Carefully considered
And laid out
Your orchestrated final exit

I felt it sharply
With accompanying finality
Sad for losing you
And stepping closer to greater pains

Stumbling Forward 2005 – 2008

We bid you farewell
In God's presence
We accepted your life as good
And your death as blessing

Goodbye Grandma Huff
I loved you and am humbly reminded
Of my own place
In God's passing universe

Take my prayers to that better Place
Walk in His unimaginable light
Onward to Infinity
Godbless. Goodnight.

To His Purpose (10.12.08)

The season of change has returned
Promise hiding in cool nights
Searching for a still place to emerge
Unfolding to some hidden purpose

In this time, the natural world slows
To a resting heartbeat,
Taking its final breaths
Before plunging into winter

The slowing cadence of the night's voices
Mirrors the coming stillness,
A harbinger of the quiet,
All must face

Alone with my thoughts,
The blown leaf scratching on steps, calls to me
Echoed by siblings unfallen,
Caressing the wind in the tree

The soft bugle announces the coming change,
A quiet and insuppressible power,
Introduces it without ceremony
One more passing in a world of passings

Stumbling Forward 2005 – 2008

Receding and progressing silently,
This change eludes my understanding
But invites my witness and, if possible, my embrace
Like the cricket, slowly dying to his purpose

In Your Space (10.12.08)

Sometimes I sit in your room
Alone
The house empty and quiet
Your space ordered
In your own haphazard way
Orbiting two centers
Your things lay where last touched
The monitor holding gravity
Over a world of inhabitants
Worshipping the shrine of technology
Your bed anchoring
The artistic and intellectual
Elements of your space

Your growing has been
Magical to watch
The evolution of a self
To whom I've been spectator
And accidental architect
There's such history in your future
It takes true silence
To fall into these recognitions

Stumbling Forward 2005 – 2008

Disturbing nothing
I survey the artifacts
Of a boy's path to manhood
Your blanket tattered and aged,
With you since birth
Your toys, out of sight, but still present
A monument to something
You're not ready to let go
Guitars, reflecting the artist
Strewn about in a kind of rock ballet

I see no randomness
There is purpose to this disorder
Your being reflected
In each item in its place
Your life's fingerprint
Unique and traceable
Lying before me

Closing my eyes
I can see you
Moving between these stations
Picking at your guitar, moving your mouse
Reading Atlas Shrugged on your bed
Painting figures at your desk

Traveler

Precious, these moments, memories
Steps I've witnessed, a life built
Unfolding
Here, in your space

Steps Toward Conversion
2009 – 2016

Stumbling Forward 2005 – 2008

Forty (02.11.09)

The days have carried me
Four decades to now
Moments past
Now held in memory

This whirlwind called life
Has swept me along
Hurling me,
To unknown destinations

Looking back
The randomness holds more meaning
Lines drawn
Across time's connect-the-dots

Tonight's wind, angry and urgent
Reminds me of the tidal swells
Rocking stout ships, they taunt me,
daring me to brave their violent ambitions

Though I rest safely
Behind the walls and thin facades
I know the power circling my house,
Invisible forces molding my world

Traveler

Their expectant grasp
Waiting to embrace what I offer the world
And perhaps demand,
That which I do not

Forty years have forged me
Hardened me to Time's temper
Still youthfully impressionable,
Despite this firm carapace

The night blows change upon me
Tomorrow's first step
Pulling me,
Toward unknown earth

I am ready, but not impervious
I am receptive; but not blind
His purpose to me bequeathed,
A destiny stitched upon my life

I welcome the gusts
And the dark howling.
Offering myself to their shaping,
I pray for the blessings of a worthy life

Stumbling Forward 2005 – 2008

First Steps (09.02.09)

You lay there, quiet, unmoving
The soft hum of the vent
Counting the moments.
I move from impassive to teary
Wondering, worrying, remembering

The confusion of sadness grips me
One moment holding gratitude,
It quickly slips away, leaving grief
Happy memories fade to harsh realities
So it goes

There is no comfort
In the waiting room
No happy endings,
Though their absence seems a necessity,
A rite of passage to a maturity I do not want

Sandwiched between hope and despair
I watch you, searching for signs
Can you hear us?
Are you already watching
From a better place?

Traveler

My eyes slowly follow each line, tube, wire
Crisscrossing you in a life-sustaining net
Your body, frail and limp,
Now appearing so very empty
Without your presence

As I return to the designated place,
Eyes search my face for some sign of hope
A new discovery that I cannot offer
I grimly hold my tears,
knowing there is only one path from this room

Stumbling Forward 2005 – 2008

Unready (09.02.09)

The days roll past
Marching us closer
To an acceptance
For which we are not ready.
The acronyms, measurements, readings
All conspire to take you
Stealthy thieves leaving nothing
But broken hearts.
I watch it all like a movie
I've already seen.
Each character tragic in her own way
The supporting cast on cue
Roll the camera on our realization
There was no battle.
His invisible hand
Setting in motion our darkest fears
Long before we suspected
Nothing but prayer remains
And the feeble attempt to fill the space
He once inhabited.

Fleeting Essence (09.04.09)

I saw the red moon waning,
A final farewell to the man we'd known before
Passing in the night, he left us for brighter pastures
The emptiness bites but solace emerges from unearned faith

As my mind wanders, dreamlike, across memories
  of knowing
I see you standing there, hat on, smiling devilishly
At a joke waiting for me to get it,
Knowing I'll catch up, eventually

I'll be years unraveling the small mysteries
Buried in snippets of conversation
Hidden wisdom you left for me,
All the better for slow discovery

The stories will live on
Told often by loving fans
Enabling us to cherish the fleeting essence
Of the time we shared

Stumbling Forward 2005 – 2008

You Stood There (09.05.09)

You stood there
Backlit by sunshine
Watson hat on your head
Smiling, patiently
You mentioned something
About the confluence of the universe,
My own fog blurring the rest
Your wizened eyes sparkled knowingly
And though you spoke no more,
I recognized a truth I can't remember
Then you turned
Walking in that golden place
Between longing and hope
Leaving me in darkness
I woke, disoriented, wondering
Unable to grasp the moment before
Sally said she was changed,
Her world inside and out made different
I considered your smile and realized
It was the best comfort you could offer
Then the day called
And I walked into another light

Traveler

No Longer There (09.05.09)

I walked toward the creek
Hoping to find you skipping stones
Or explaining frog behavior
Passing the doorway of your falling
My heart stopped as my mind raced –
You lay there bleeding, moaning
Your own passing ringing in your ears
And you were gone, whispering into the breeze.
The corn stands at attention
Somehow somber and sincere
As I find myself at the creek,
Small and drifting slowly
It reflects you and the simple things you loved
Unable to mourn, it moves on stoically
Then I see it, a great blue heron
Walking among the grasses, tall, majestic
Suddenly spreading its wings
And launching toward the horizon
Taking with it my thoughts of you
And the prayers I repeat silently
Until you are no longer there

More Remains (09.05.09)

So many thoughts
Crowd my saddened mind
Tiny pieces of lives lived
And the one ahead
Reading, writing, praying
There seems a steady purge
Of profound energies
Converging on these moments
Until it seems I might empty this vessel
Yet more remains
Welling up to spill
Into the world around me
We grieve for loss
But it is the loss of ourselves
A piece made whole then shattered
By removing one element
Leaving us to rebuild
With a new combination of parts
An apprenticeship to our own life
With no right answers or blueprint
Only a vague sense of direction
And His invisible hand guiding us

Gone (09.05.09)

"It's gone," you whispered
Following your eyes across the field of beans
I saw the empty place
Where my dreaming tree once stood
Taken by pragmatism and economy
The broad branches replaced by absence and a clear view
The symbol of two other passings,
It seems darkly poetic
That its disappearance coincides
With Roy's departure
The otherworldly tree stood stoutly hopeful
Capturing my imagination over years of changing seasons
Its brooding presence spiritually tied
To my wandering imagination
One of few symbols
Which I've claimed for my own
It's loss troubles me
Mirroring other losses
And the portion of innocence taken
With each one

Stumbling Forward 2005 – 2008

For Madison *at Roy's Passing* (09.07.09)

I read your words
And see a quiet sadness
A confused sense of loss
Trying to reconcile faith
With an acute pain
The mysterious with the known
Expressing your hurt
Gives me a window
To the innocent perspective
Of a time I cannot recall
Still, I relish your thoughts
The process by which you define yourself
And I hope you feel it
Embrace the unseen powers
At work in your life
Unknowable but present
So much left to experience
This is a moment to remember
And cherish
A passing for all of us
In our own way

Play it Again (09.11.09)

You looked at me, tears welling
The pain of my revelation burning
Your father's passing fresh on your heart
This week should be about you
Guilty as charged
My selfishness could not be restrained
Hating myself for being human
I watched you drive away
Fresh anger welling within
Even now, distance is small comfort
My demons seem loud, prominent
I love you intensely and selfishly
Even after almost 20 years
I seem unable to reconcile the two
What brought me here?
My own fragile limitations
Seem pathetic
But remain stubbornly real
Now I sit alone
The only one concerned with any of this
Already knowing how it will end

Stumbling Forward 2005 – 2008

As you wait for me to talk myself through
Finally rolling over,
Contentedly forgetting it ever occurred

I See You There (07.01.10)

I know you are gone
But I see you in many things
The tower over which you labored
Standing as a monument
To that off-center perspective
You embodied
Your room
An odd collection of photos
Personal and not
Ordered in your own mysterious pattern
The quiet creek
Full of insects, oblivious
To your passing
The dark eave covering
That place you fell
Your chair, now occupied
By your grandchildren
The pictures, videos, tapes, and CD's –
Recording what you loved
And much that inspired you
The countless people
Who knew you in their way

Stumbling Forward 2005 – 2008

I see you there
And hope someone will see me
In half as many places

Greatest Strength (09.11.09)

The fall sun seems softer
Gently warming the quiet day
Chattering cicadas call out
Announcing the season's passing
My loneliness seems complete
I feel disconnected,
From everything
There is small comfort in the blue sky
My own cloudiness pervasive
Midnight Oil plays in the background
Their anthem for the aborigines
Reminding me again of Sally
And her brief encounter in New York
Circa 1988
I search for an answer
To my own complexities
But realize the searching only brings more
There is something to be said
For letting go
A notion seemingly impossible
For my introspective self
But I know I will

Stumbling Forward 2005 – 2008

As I've done a hundred times before
Escalation simply not an option
I see you, bright and happy
Not a care
Again the little girl
Following the day with simple joy
Unburdened by my musings
Or any expectation of the minutes ahead
It is truly a gift
My eyes open, Stevie Wonder calling,
Returning me to the moment
As I realize that letting go
Shows the greatest strength

Shadows of Summer (09.14.09)

The shadows of summer
Cast themselves
Across the shortened days
Reminding us of moments lost
And the march of time

Too soon
The changes come upon us
Little we've done
Can prepare us
For the long nights ahead

Stumbling Forward 2005 – 2008

Looking for Contemplation (01.28.10)

Months have passed
Without a word
Moved by nothing
My pen has lain dormant
Words from my past
Always feel familiar
And foreign
Emotions return
But I still feel I wasn't there
These pages hold such a collection
Moments from yesterday
Captured in a thousand syllables

I sit here, drink in hand
Resting quietly and looking
For contemplation
Redemption seems elusive
For a fickle soul
My mind floats, aimlessly
Grasping at mental straws
Amid the collective challenges
Calling my mind home
I love the edge I feel

Traveler

Perhaps the purest sensation
Juxtaposed between the night's callings

Sally is back
The familiar call
Breaking the spell
The urgent has returned
With the necessity of dinner

Stumbling Forward 2005 – 2008

The Span of Time (07.01.10)

The evening quietly descends
The last sounds of the day
Accompany my solitary journey
Reading old words
Transports me to moments lost
I pause and realize
They aren't lost if I remember
It seems impossible
To grasp the span of time
Collected in my mind
Though my words cross
But a portion of the expanse

To retrace such paths is a gift
I can feel it all again
With the slightest words
The softest syllables
The hawk cries
As if calling me to another recollection
The urgency of the present
And moving within it
Can be a lonely trip

Traveler

But there is satisfaction
In stumbling along the old trails again

Stumbling Forward 2005 – 2008

With Macy (01.11.11)

"Are you happy?" I asked
"Yes"
"How do you know?"
"Because I have dance tonight."

The warm moment
Transported me to David's words
"Hold on to your robust innocence."
The simple joys
Unencumbered by the day's distractions
No bills, or wars, or crimes
Encroaching on her happy priorities
Talk of dance, hip hop and ballet
Nothing more, nothing less
No worry to stain her joy
It would be hard to ask
For anything more.
Give my baby impervious joy
To match her robust innocence.
She told me once that she is naïve –
That's ok
I think of my dark meanderings
And feel shame

Traveler

At my surrender to complexity
She is young, beautiful, pure
God bless her.

Stumbling Forward 2005 – 2008

John D. (03.12.11)

Your legacy echoes across a century
Those triumphs and failings
Resonate deep within me.
Excoriated by a jealous society,
You carved a path unmatched –
Altering the fabric of our country.
I cannot find blame or jealousy
Only admiration
For one driven by faith.
Yours was a difficult road,
Beyond my comprehension.
I see the same forces alive today
Harping the same tune
The takers are alive and well.
It's so much easier to take
Than to build.
Easier to tear down
Than craft an original path.
Our obsessive natures haven't changed
We want someone to blame,
Disasters, failures, losses
It's always the fault of another.

Traveler

You walked your path,
Never bending
To the wills of lesser men.
Your conquest of the world
Awesome to behold
As you moved mountains –
That singular drive
Which changed the world.
Moved by your story,
I envy your resolve –
That endless store of self-assurance.
Though I don't aspire to your challenges,
Your life is a model.
Deliberate and true
With iron self-discipline.
A life, a legacy
To be admired.

Stumbling Forward 2005 – 2008

Time Well Spent (08.24.11)

Your glance arrested me
With its tender vulnerability
At once fragile and determined,
It conveyed the quiet secrets
Held in two decades of marriage
Saying nothing, yet everything
Your eyes tell the story
And I understand
I love you, I need you, I believe in you
I trust you
You bring something I can't find alone
Time has a way of forming something
You never knew existed
It is no casual creation
But the hard-earned discovery
Of things beyond yourself
Subtle yet direct
It cannot be given
But must be built
In the small, laborious steps
Of thousands of days
It's nothing you deserve
But everything you dreamed

These Days (08.30.12)

These days
The world's changing
Strikes me acutely
The black & white living
Of my youth,
Long gone amid the grays
Of the life I live
The long pattern of my fatherhood
Is fading, changing, evolving
Though it always was
I feel it more fully
Than I can remember
My place in the world
Shifting
Into something unknown
This new identity foreign,
But not uncomfortable
The purpose remains,
Reformulated,
But still profound.
In the gaping hole,
Of times devoted to little ones,

Stumbling Forward 2005 – 2008

Rises a new life
Broader though more focused
My path even more clear
As my giving evolves

Northwind (08.08.14)

I've never belonged to a place
My life's memory
A twisting, rushing river
Of times, people, places
Comfort abounded in change
Born of perpetual transition
My roots spread quickly
But never deep
Now, here, I feel a sense of belonging
Just starting to recognize
The beauty of the familiar
The short lines of my drive
A bird or two now familiar
Those towering pines
And their disheveled shadows
Each an element of my home
Inside, the changing appearances
Can't mask the memories
Is a life built in ten years?
These walls have seen it
Each window holds a view
Across all seasons

Stumbling Forward 2005 – 2008

The sad, hopeless visions
Side by side with the bright possibilities
The moments have paraded here
Over the distance of time
I never wanted to stay
Never believed that I would belong,
Could belong
But the years impose change
A place can reach the heart
And though I may not walk here always
I feel what it means to belong

Loud with Memories (12.10.14)

The night is loud
With memories
Moments that could not be held
Yet linger in those softer parts of me
Time continues
To work her magic
Smoothing my edges
And pulling me further
Into unknown territory
I feel an intense longing
To stare deeply into the past
Until my eyes drip with recollection

As my days change
And I'm challenged
by my own evolution
I struggle with a sense of loss
Lost moments and opportunities
Places where I wasn't present
Too busy gazing elsewhere
This path, a fool's journey
And regret not my style

Stumbling Forward 2005 – 2008

Reconciling it takes intention
And open arms accepting
Renewal in a fresh tomorrow

Still the Same (04.04.15)

My words
Jump off the pages
Taking me back
To moments long past

Familiar feelings, thoughts, and sentiments
Fill my being
As I tune-in
To each sensation

My days march on
New challenges emerge
But looking closer
I see the past's shadow

Though my face shifts
Under Time's touch
The demons I face
are still the same

Questions unanswered
Longings unfulfilled
Strivings unreached
Hopes unrelenting

Stumbling Forward 2005 – 2008

The quest continues
And though the objective
Remains obscured
I begin to understand

There is only one arrival
All else, simply the journey
A collection of adventures
Chronicled in the book of our lives

The geography may change
New characters may appear
But the hopes, doubts, and dreams
Are still the same

On we go
Until the going is done
Growing, evolving, and looking back
Only to see that we're still the same

Surrender to Complexity (04.04.15)

The noise accumulates,
Collected like refuse
From a week-end in the yard
Each pile growing as we rake or prune
But these collections
Aren't easily hauled away
We build our piles of commitments
Responsibilities that follow us
Through hurried days
More begets more
And on we go, gathering
Until we are consumed
Worry, fear, and doubt become mainstays
As we struggle to cope
Where did our time go?
Where is the joy?
The days roll on
And our bags fill
Like the rooms in our house
Lined with the things
We had to have
Ambition turned to hoarding

Stumbling Forward 2005 – 2008

As we push further
Into the never-ending cycle
Wondering what ever made us decide
To surrender to complexity

I Weep *at Ben's passing* (04.29.15)

I weep for all that you were
and all that you might have been

I weep for all who loved you
and the emptiness never to be filled

I weep for the lives you touched
though you never knew

I weep for my self
and the ache I feel in your passing

I weep for the time lost
never to be recovered

I weep for your empty saddle
and the trails not ridden

There are no answers,
only questions, doubts, fears.

There is no consolation.
Only the steps forward through grief
into this new life you've left us to live.

Stumbling Forward 2005 – 2008

Do Your Best (05.27.15)

Do your best.
Her parting words hung in the air,
and my mind,
as I fumbled through the dark.

The night was heavy upon us
and her words seemed to flow
from another world, not fitting the moment
yet profoundly prescient.

The nature and definition
of a person's best is ephemeral,
changing, wraithlike with the moment
there and gone silently.

These words were encouragement.
A prayer for a troubled heart
and an admonishment
to a challenged soul.

Earlier that day, I spoke of adversity
as a single obstacle.
She reminded me of its true nature
as an enduring companion.

Traveler

I paused in the silence of the night.
Considering her words as I walked to the door.
In the hazy, half-awake moment,
I felt the compassion, and forgiveness.

You are not alone.
You don't have to be perfect.
We will find a way.
Do your best.

Stumbling Forward 2005 – 2008

If Only (05.27.15)

If only....
the day were a little longer

If only...
I felt a little better

If only...
I had more money

We spend our lives waiting

for the right moment

for the ideal circumstances

for permission

If only...
I was better

Hoping for that perfect alignment

If only...
I was luckier

Dreaming of possibilities

Traveler

a better place down the road

If only...
I made better choices

Searching for signs of relief

in a world designed to test us

If only...
She loved me

Waiting

If only...
I had remembered to live

Stumbling Forward 2005 – 2008

Of Our Own Making (05.27.15)

The turbines hum
in a rhythmic melody
engulfing me, embracing me
in a steady buzz, constant.

Air flowing, a mechanical wind
invisibly present.

These are the elements of escape
thirty thousand feet above,
surrounded in isolation.

Those other noises subside,
lost in the steadiness of this
more demanding presence.

In this aluminum nirvana,
we feel a more elemental existence.

Nothing in our control with
the most limited of choices –
we're shuttled along within another's grasp.

It mirrors our broader existence,
players in another's game, but

Traveler

the finite nature of this world
bears our limitations honestly.

No pretense of control or influence –
here, we simply are.

Freed thus, the mind wanders
in and around the known, eventually
settling into the unknown.

The might-be of our life.
It is quiet, and possible.
Above the clouds, all seems possible.

On we go, steady, forward.

Flying toward a sunrise
of our own making.

Stumbling Forward 2005 – 2008

Shared on a Summer's Eve (06.10.15)

You stood there,
golden and beautiful.
Poised for flight into the night.
Innocent and hopeful,
you listened
to yet another rambling
set of platitudes.
You've always been a good sport,
accepting my nuggets of wisdom.
Whether or not they were wanted.
I suppose that's love.
Listening even when you don't want to.
I once heard a song,
saying that love is:
watching someone die.
That song reminds me
of the final moments with your grandpa.
But I see love in the thousand
little nothings, we give every day.
Your patient, open face,
listening, smiling, and thinking.
Considering each utterance,

Traveler

as if your father might give you the secret.
I will always try; you may always listen.
But these are places you will need to walk.
Alone.
We both know it,
Though, it won't discourage my efforts.

Stumbling Forward 2005 – 2008

Your Words (07.03.15)

I want to go there
but I feel unequal to the task
you travel to a depth
seemingly beyond my range
the rich texture
of your words
inspiring, nourishing
sometimes I feel that I wrote them
but your signature remains
reminding me
that my notion is only an aspiration
taking me to that other place
where calm lightness
holds my heaviest thoughts
and I emulate the you
I remember
intensely introspective
even while giving it all away

Liberty (07.03.15)

we, living now,
cannot deserve the countless sacrifices

each is beyond our worthiness
only the gift remains

Liberty bought with blood and self
a mere idea turned into our reality

a hope and a dream that we've forgotten
taken for granted in a world of mine and yours

the question comes across the decades,
what will you do to earn this gift?
how will you justify the price paid?

the roads we've traveled
and the paths before us

spring from byways carved long ago
ours is only one leg of a bigger journey

with an uncertain destination
freedom is a fragile gift

delicate in our hands,
we seem bent on giving it away

but our fathers saw something bigger,
chose to believe

and invested in this future we are living
these are blessings

we now possess
whether or not we see them

regardless of our choice to embrace or reject them
Liberty is ours,

to cherish, to enjoy, to protect
the challenges remain

there is a price to be paid
today, tomorrow, always

Uncertain (07.12.15)

The world is changing
a condition that's never changed
though I feel it distinctly
this new place
where the old hopes no longer apply
people, places, things, shifting
morphing toward a tomorrow
not visible
but these are only sensations
those deceitful feelings
distracting from the moment
trapping us between melancholy
and a deeper happiness
taunting us with a life lived
when there is much life yet to live
the thoughtful cast upon those rocks
even as the ship is sailing
toward the horizon
it is a necessary path
the ebb and flow of comfort
among the world known and unknown
too much contemplation

Stumbling Forward 2005 – 2008

fosters loose footing,
an imbalance
when grounding is what we seek
it is there, in and on those jagged edges
you know the way, instinctively
innocently doubting
even as you cast about for certainty
the old hopes are moving on
giving way to new possibility
regardless of your readiness
this is happening
your grip will not hold
and the way before you
is the only answer
these ruminations but shadows
of that part of you that has already moved on

Gone (08.06.15)

Your bed lies empty
Your fans are still
This morning came
And you were gone

The differences can be measured
In the tiniest increments
A closed door, shoes on the floor
The day's routine, all no more

For nearly 19 years
Your life has led to this moment
But knowing it would arrive
Is small comfort

The quiet morning
Reflects my conflicted melancholy
Sadness and joy
Conspiring to confuse my senses

The obvious loss grips first
Our casual moments the first victim
Dinner, movies, drives, and ice cream
The small joys we shared

Stumbling Forward 2005 – 2008

Moving deeper, your questions
The daily discoveries and conversations
Your intellectual curiosity
And force of thought

Sometimes agreeing, sometimes not
Pushing me, yet still open
Innocent and certain
As only youth can be

Seeking
Sharing
Growing
Gone

I miss the boy building armies
And castles in the sky
Amid awe with endless wonder
Adventuring in fantastic imagination

Battles fought and won
You've marched on
Leaving our house silent
Bereft of your singular specialness

The future before you
Another matter altogether

Traveler

The loss is mine
Opportunity is yours

My melancholy retreats
From the joy of watching you
Spread your wings, launching into tomorrow
And the world awaiting your discoveries

The parting necessary
And my heart full
Considering the memory
Of the first moments in your new life

Subdued anxiety
Hid behind equally restrained joy
Fearing seeming too happy
Your eyes twinkled with anticipation

Now ready to stretch your legs
Waiting patiently
"I love you"
Now, let me go

Pride, the word little captures
Such satisfaction in seeing
Your confident certitude
Blazing through your being

Stumbling Forward 2005 – 2008

But pride and joy
Balance the sadness
Of this new chapter
For all of us

The days ahead give us
New places to grow
Together, then separately
Yours is now yours alone

The old, comfortable ways
Will shift in different directions
As they should, as they must
We'll be what you need us to be

Missing what has past, the tears must fall
While embracing what's to come
Watching you take your place
In life's greater conversation

Vulnerable (09.06.15)

The written word
Reveals something more
A deeper story
Giving voice to your being

The words stand alone
No tone or inflection
No visual queues
Only the reader's interpretation

In those words
Lies complete exposure
A vulnerability
As deep as anything physical

To write is to put yourself
Squarely at the feet
Of the broader world
Laid bare for all

In your words
You invite disapproval
Disagreement and scorn
Arrows sharp and true

Stumbling Forward 2005 – 2008

Yet, in the vulnerable
Lies a deeper connection
A place to join
With those invested

To be vulnerable
Is to be true
To a deeper self
And those seeking your words

Imperfect (12.19.15)

The rough edges endear,
fostering a comfort
grounded in the real

Unsymmetrical shapes
forming the outline
of a life, gritty, imperfect

Winding, weaving
fluid and indirect
our journey builds

daily, foundational
to an unseen completion
that never occurs

Unfathomable, incomprehensible
it is ours for a moment
then lost, imperfect

Holding more tightly,
Moments slip through quickly,
defying hope for control

Stumbling Forward 2005 – 2008

Striving, seeking, hoping, and dreaming
planning and forging
yet still tossed along, imperfect

Predestined to end
we play our part in the time we have
giving, living, loving, imperfect

Traveler

Sharing Silver (25 years together) (12.22.15)

In the half light of the morning
I glimpse you
Fully formed and beautiful
Reminiscent of that girl I knew
Now evolved to something more

Youthful, radiant eyes, both wise and innocent
Reveal a life lived across the spectrum of experience
And though I love the girl you were,
I love more fully the woman you've become.

Time molds us like water through a canyon,
Carving those edges physically, emotionally, spiritually
Crafting us into complete versions of ourselves.
Full, rich, complex; the depths present facets
Worthy of exploration. Compelling and fascinating.

The years, the moments, bring us
To one threshold after another
Beyond which lies the next version of our self.
Seeing you here, now, I remember
Many thresholds we've crossed together
And the versions who emerged.

Stumbling Forward 2005 – 2008

These doorways open to our life, together
And individually
No longer singular but defined in a plurality
Reflective of our commitment.
The waters of life moving us forward,
Sometimes calm, often turbulent,
We've navigated all of it, together.
Again and again and again.

Today, the full beauty of your experience,
Maturity, and grace,
Inspires a richness of affection,
A depth of emotion I never thought possible.
The eyes and hearts of our children
Reflect this lasting love
As I recognize your faithful spirit
Embracing all that I am
And forgiving all that I am not.

Tomorrow is a gift, forged from the
Countless today's we've shared.
I relish the moments to come even as
I cherish what has passed,
There is no reference point as we long
Ago traveled toward the unknown.

Traveler

But I know the way ahead promises
Beauty and discovery.
The rest, I leave to the faith we share
And the belief that there
Is purpose in our journey together.

Spent (06.09.16)

Past fatigue is an edge,
A place where the body falters, completely spent
Here lies a fullness
A satisfaction
The self-emptying, a corporal gift
Time makes such depletion difficult
But capacity remains
Pushing to the precipice,
You can go no further
This is enough
Nothing else necessary
Revel in your time
It won't wait

Macy (07.04.16)

Everyone is home
And you slipped quietly
Into the background
Of course, yours
Is a quiet strength
An unassumed beauty
Wise and pragmatic
There is a glorious efficiency
In your endearing emotions
You are my baby
The last.
Powerfully intelligent,
Your youth belies
Your depth of perspective
We share a love
That appreciates winks and glances
A mutual comfort
In saying nothing
Content to simply be near
I know we're heading
Into unknown days
They promise delight

Stumbling Forward 2005 – 2008

As you bless us with
Your own experience,
Shadowing paths already walked

Forgive me Grandma (07.04.16)

"Yes, she has a dark side."
I replied
Immediately regretting
That deep step into
Purposeless conversation
Instantly feeling the betrayal
Somehow believing it would vindicate
But knowing that guilt
Was now my only verdict
How tedious is the derision of the inane
Sucking the last element of humanity
While magnifying its imperfections
The words brought gloom
And though I pouted and pushed
There was no retreat
Please forgive my smallness
This insidious failing
Meaningless in the wide world
But heavy on my soul
The spirit of conversation
A damning judgment

Stumbling Forward 2005 – 2008

On my own
And a dark disrespect
Cast across your grave

The Afternoon (07.06.16)

The afternoon welcomed
My restless return
For I had already betrayed
Morning's bright expectations
The holes we find
Seem endlessly varied
Accessible, dark, endless
Waiting patiently
For us to crawl within
So willing
We are victims
Of our own indifference
An unwillingness
To hold tightly
To our more hopeful
Inclinations
My return brought
Its own clouds
Nothing left
But to crawl out

Words Unread (07.09.16)

You asked me to read to you,
I dismissed it as insincere.
You asked me to read to you,
I brushed it away as silly.
You asked me to read to you,
I rolled over to disappear in the distance.
You asked me to read to you,
I ignored you, not feeling it.

Is it a romantic notion or
Something in my voice? Both?
What prompted your request?
The long dark days
Lost inside your waking world
Create their own loneliness.
A need to connect on some other level.
With the one person most needed.

I didn't see it.
The clarity eluded me.
All my introspection and deep perspective
Lost in the selfishly consuming
Noise of me, I, mine.

Traveler

We are such victims
Of our own inclinations
Perspectives twisted by need.
Greedily we expect more
And miss those chances to give.

I am no exception.
Staring me in the face
Was the path for which I'd prayed.
A return to something we once had.
I thought it was gone but the road
Had only turned.
You offered the map,
But I was too busy being lost
To accept your directions.

Shift (08.04.16)

I feel it, subtle and mysterious
My heart adrift
My mind wandering
I'm in a shift

The days move in mirrored circles
But I'm walking somewhere new
The way unfolding
I'm in a shift

The patterns recognizable
But somehow more distinct
Reformed to something new
I'm in a shift

Simultaneously larger and smaller
I see new horizons
Pushing against contracting movements
I'm in a shift

Summoned to a greater
Version of myself
The world is opening
I'm in a shift

Traveler

No more certain
Than before
The questions remain
I'm in a shift

The moments beyond
Are expansive, sweeping, profound
Showing me something more
I'm in a shift

Comforted and encouraged
I walk boldly
Toward the signs
I'm in a shift

Stumbling Forward 2005 – 2008

Emma Stone (08.04.16)

The evening is young
And U2 reminds me
Of those moody moments
That only an Irish youth
Might truly comprehend
I sit thinking, wondering
You comfort me
With a smooth edge
Full and sophisticated
Your flavor takes me
To another place
I stole your formula
But now claim it as mine
And you visit me
Like a genie from her bottle
Robust, sensual, magical
I smile as I consider
Your passing
It is a guilty pleasure
We share
And I know you can't stay
But I treasure this moment

Traveler

Brief, ephemeral, intoxicating
Emma Stone

Stumbling Forward 2005 – 2008

I'm Sorry (pictures on the piano) (08.04.16)

Your pictures
Frame these moments
Looking eternally in my direction
But those times are gone
Only your image remains
And I'm saddened
To never have known you
As I am now
Where I am now
What might we have discussed?
Had I put myself fully
In that moment,
Would there have been
Something more?
Would that I could
Have shared myself with you
I feel that I was half-formed
When we last spoke
For that, I am sorry
It is nothing I can take back
Simply something
I couldn't give

Traveler

I see you now
Smiling, forever in your eyes
And I want that moment back
I want you to see me
As I see you now

Stumbling Forward 2005 – 2008

Lost in a Shifting Shadow (08.07.16)

That ray of sunlight
Peers between the trees
A maple-tinged beam
Highlighting the morning dew
On yesterday's fresh-cut grass
The glint of tiny gnats
Flicker in the light
Their wings moving them
To an unseen destination

Sunday morning in my yard
A micro reflection
Of the universal view
On our frenetic world
The sun rising higher
Until its fingers touch me
From over the treetops
No longer hidden, I sit
Revealed in the day's light
Squinting over a brightened
Expanse of moist green blades
Stretching to my sight's limits

Traveler

Turning, my shadow appears
Pan-like across the bricks
Trailing my impression
Like a pantomime
Telling its own silent story
Now, even my pen casts a shadow
Reminding me of traces
Seen or unseen, left upon
The pages of our life
Made permanent
Through the music
That will always remember this moment

Am I crazy?
All I remember is thinking
I want to live like this,
Free, feeling –
Existing in this moment fully
Living this fantasy
Of words and sensations
Purposeless and profound
In their Polaroid snapshot
Of a few moments
Mine and mine alone
Until they're gone
Lost in a shifting shadow

Stumbling Forward 2005 – 2008

Passing (08.07.16)

The thread glinted
Caught in the light
And then gone
Silky strand. Ephemeral.
As mysterious
As the cardinal's call
Framing this moment
There is a tear
Edging from my eye
Holding on,
Glistening, not ready to fall
As temporary as the web
Lost in the sunshine
It is all passing
In the prevailing seconds
Marching to another edge
A threshold to the next
No return, just passing
These are the moments
Not to be held
Only experienced
Do we see them?

Traveler

Or lose ourselves
Looking beyond
Missing the glint, the call, the tear,
Those few seconds
And all they reveal

Joy (08.07.16)

There, now I feel it
Transported by
Words, music, light
Basking in warm brightness
God's radiance
Why wouldn't we worship the sun?
What a powerful reflection
Of His unseen glory
It is not easy to get here
Trancelike, still
Yet sitting on the edge
Of something more
This place cannot be fabricated
It is a gift
Happening despite
My own unworthiness
The breeze whispers comfort
Reminding me
It is not something
To be earned
As with God's Grace
All I can do

Traveler

Is receive it, humbly
Reveling in the moment
Allowing it to be
Holding it as I may
Then letting it go

Beyond (09.05.16)

"The sun will be no more"
From *Moby's Lie Down in Darkness*
Takes me away

Removing my glasses
Gifting myself with
My own edgy limitation
I walk into the melody
The outside world blurry
Out of focus, it beckons me
To a closer clarity
But I'm content
To let everything beyond my sight
Remain invisible
Lost beyond the green shroud
Of trees and grass
Lit by yellow glory
The day seems infinite
So far beyond
The finite world of my vision
The crow calls invisible and defiant
Challenging and warning
"This won't be easy"

Traveler

It's a promise I relish
Happy to savor the breeze
The Breath of God
Washing across my face
I look again wondering what lies beyond
My sight, my senses, my imagination
This humanity is so limiting
My frailties ever-present
As I seek to push farther
Returning the lenses to my eyes
Reveals the world again
Where else am I blind?
What other clarities
Lay just beyond my sight?
Returning to Moby
I've taken the song for my own
A catalyst to move beyond
Embracing the sadness of passing
With the otherworldliness
Of the infinite
Recalling the gifts of my life
Focus returns
The crow departs
As that breeze whispers
"I am here"

Stumbling Forward 2005 – 2008

Remembering (09.11.16)

These are days of intense remembering
Momentous times
Held between life's calmer seconds
Dates intertwined, unrelated
But laden with significance
And sadness

The image of the towers
Smolders in my mind
Like the smoke and fire
Emanating from their mortal wounds
The banal repetition of the talking heads
Punctuating the surreal picture
Leaving a sense of the fictional
In spite of this harsh reality

I recall the world stopping
Confusion on a 24 hour,
Completely televised scale
No one sure what it meant
Or what would happen next
I stood staring at the TV
Listening, mind racing, fearing

Traveler

When they fell, my mind raced back
To my layover in Newark months before
The casual snapshot
Of those implacable towers
Bound with New York's skyline forever
Now, heaps of rubbish
Felled in moments

The uncertainty was real
A follow-on attack on the Pentagon
Fighters scrambled
Indecision gripping people, business, the world
For weeks to come
The days went by but the fear stayed
Gripping all of us
The reality of our vulnerability
Bared in this violation
And then we rained hell on them
Any and all we could find
While the fear slowly passed

Eight years later
That day faded to a more personal loss
As we waited for Roy to die
Felled near his own tower

Stumbling Forward 2005 – 2008

Those last moments
Of fear and uncertainty
His labored breathing controlled
By the most impersonal machine
The tubes and wires
Connecting his empty body
With life-giving technology
But it wasn't life
Only a collection of organs
Barely functioning

We watched as his breaths slowed
The robotic sounds of the ventilator
Confirming the brutal nature
Of this form of sustenance
Tears and sniffles interrupting
With a more human touch
I knew you were gone
Long before your last breath
Your empty shell going through
Manufactured motions
Until the switch was moved to 'Off'
Then the world slowed
Each painful second taking us closer
To the death of your body

Traveler

A finality that felt heavier
Than anything I have ever felt

Today, I remember both inflection points
The distant impact of 9/11
The immediate devastation of Roy's death
Forever imprinted
On these September days

Fall's Leaves (11.01.16)

Bullet proof
The last fleeting thought
Before the world crashes down

Therein lies the fear
Comfort leads to hubris
Punishment follows

Harboring such superstition
Undermines the precarious balance
Of self-assurance and humility

Such is the paradox of our world
Confidence so essential
Rests just before the fall of pride

To be fearless
Is to fly freely
To move without obstruction

Our life can't tolerate such fearlessness
A freedom which overwhelms
Our capacity to believe

Traveler

Instead we twist about
Like fall's leaves still hanging in the tree
Waiting to be blown to the ground

Stumbling Forward 2005 – 2008

Called to More (11.01.16)

How do I look at all of it
And not feel overwhelmed?
Layers upon nuances
Rolled over possibilities

It is said that focus
Yields great success
But I find myself
Enthralled with many successes

The truth is
I feel called to more
This world's measure
Seems thin, incomplete

Of what are you capable?
Defined by title, duty, brand
We lower ourselves
To the highest place offered

Waiting to be picked
Our gifts gather dust
Their great expanse
Narrowed to the space of a cubicle

Traveler

Great work can be wrought
In many places
It is the forge of our mind
That forms our shackles

The signs are there
If we only open our eyes
Our calling written
Across life's backdrop

Still, we miss it
Too busy checking another box
On a list
We didn't create

Stumbling Forward 2005 – 2008

Your Greatest Gift (11.01.16)

All that you are
The hopes and dreams
The words and deeds
The ideas, insights, and perspectives
In the visible
And the invisible
Your mark on the world
Imprints left on land
Mind and heart
No one person
Fully aware
Only God knows
The choices made
The victories and the losses
The art and the happiness
In being present
And leaving it alone
The smiles lost in time
A billion expressions
Touching untold souls
A universe forever changed
Simply by your passing

Traveler

Living is the giving
Of your greatest gift

Stumbling Forward 2005 – 2008

Seasons of Life (11.26.16)

This season holds me
Tightly gripped in Time's embrace
The days passing
In the sweep of my grand epic
Each anniversary
Takes us further
Away from those hopeful intentions
While bringing us closer
To that final discovery
The moments between
Define a life
In all the simple complexities
Compressed into those four letters
I see the threads
Woven across our stories
A history apart from
Other fabrics
Yet still intertwined
Into the cosmic throw
Cast across centuries
My children grow,
My parents age
While I cast about

Traveler

Searching for my place
In between
Growing and aging
In my own quiet way
In the winsome silence
Of these holiday mornings
I feel it all intensely
Not sadly, but fully
As if surveying a map
With everything in its place
The broader image
Revealing itself
Along the boundaries and roadways
Marked like tiny cities
Milestones and byways
Outlining the scope,
The breadth of a full life
Separate but still within
The bigger picture
Grateful for those points of light
I turn to the darker places
As yet unseen, untraveled
And feel the full weight of my Faith
Comforting and calling me
To a life not yet lived

The Moments Before (12.24.16)

In the moments before
Light's first break
Silence is an old friend
Steady, present, patient

With dawn's sweeping presence
The world changes
No longer melancholy with sleep
But vibrant with possibility

Such is the cycle of birth and rebirth
Today is that edge
The cusp of our anticipation
For our Savior's return

In spite of my own flailing faith
And flawed smallness
I dream vastly
In the hope of my God

In the moments before
I hold tightly to unearned Grace
And the forgiveness
Of His eternal love

Traveler

The day ahead
Will distract and delight
Disappoint and stress
But mostly, leave me searching

For He rests beyond my sight
Promising eternity
And asking me for more
More love, more faith, more

These moments before
Remind me of other expectations
My own children, my own dreams,
And the joys dancing at those thresholds

The gift is beyond imagining
And the limits of understanding
Knowingly unequal to the call, I accept it and Him
Forgiving myself along the way

These are my moments
My sunrise, my God
And my humbled self
Unworthy, but desperately accepting

Stumbling Forward 2005 – 2008

The End is Near (12.24.16)

All edges and endings
This is life
Always nearing completion
Moving toward finality
In these pages
Time moves,
Marked by dates, book ends
To some arbitrary window.
Nearing another end
Brings the dark melancholy
Of loss

And therein lies the dichotomy
Around the corner,
A new beginning awaits
These are merely seasons
Passing, blending, changing
Winter's finality
Yields to spring's insistence
The start of something new
These pages will be filled
The book completed

Traveler

yet the story goes on
with that next blank page

The end is near,
as is the beginning.

Stumbling Forward 2005 – 2008

I See You *for Baby Choiniere* (12.24.16)

With little effort
Your face comes to me
Though your features remain unclear
I know it's you
We have yet to meet
Yet we are already friends
For I am bound to you
To the limits of my mortality
I will love and cherish all you are

You are mine
And I am yours
The fears, skinned knees, and bright discoveries
All lie ahead
And I pray to be there with you
Your hopes and dreams
Are mine as well
For I want it all, for you
Holding your hand
I will walk anywhere
If you'll have me

Traveler

In this way
I anticipate your arrival
Knowing and yet, not knowing you
This is the mystery
Of the heart's love
For God has called me
To be there for you
And my affections are yours
Always

There's still much time
Before we meet
But it will pass quickly
I will wait patiently
Preparing, expecting
Praying for a world worthy
Of all your future hopes
And looking forward
To being there along the way
As you turn your eyes
Toward your own horizons

Walking with Conviction
2017-2020

Not so Bold (01.10.17)

Not so bold
Am I now
Life's yoke holds me
Doubt rests upon my brow

Pride my sin
Haughty boldness
Filled my heart with desire
And brought this fear to me

The hesitation enfolds
My waking hours
Blinding me to the trees
Numbing me to the flowers

Knowing this place
I curse my quiet boasts
Look at me forging my way
A king, conqueror of distant lands

The gift you give,
Allowing me to feel
The doubt and hesitation
Reminders of what's real

Traveler

The glories of this life
Mine for a time
Lost to eternity
And Heaven sublime

You gave us life
And hard-won salvation
Even as we wander
And return abnegation

For it is in the low places
That we most realize
We cannot do this
Without Your uncompromising love

So I go forth today
Fear, doubt, and hope
Looking to You
Praying to cope

For I know
I am never alone
You are with me always
Even when I least deserve it

Walking with Conviction 2017-2020

In the Beginning (01.14.17)

In the beginning
Were thoughts and intentions
The words came later
Reluctantly
The blank pages
Mirrored a longing,
Searching progression
Toward something unseen
Unknown
Sensed yet indescribable
The first steps hesitant,
Faltering toward that horizon
Hopeful and uncertain
Plodding onward
Called to more
Then, the rush
Emotions initially
A kaleidoscope
Welling within, building
Bursting on those waiting pages
More words
More thoughts

Traveler

More questions
The pen was alive
Too slow to capture
Each frantic word
Pouring forth
Heroically attempting
A newly expressive dance
Along the lines
There was an energy
In that beginning
A desperate need
To express, to shine, to share
With no one in particular
Yet with the whole world
That first journal
Was a deep, blue ocean
Unexplored, mysterious
Full of hidden truths
And unexpressed desires
Promising salvation
The siren call came
Seducing with something new
Dangerous and alive
All the world laid bare
In possibility

There is only one beginning
The rest is journey
As the pages fill
The road is revealed
Yet the mysteries remain
One word at a time
Evolving

The Way of a Pilgrim (01.24.17)

This journey feels new
Unknown and uncertain
Formed in the union
Of reason and faith

The way seems very familiar
The comfortable place of return
Yet fresh twists, and texture
Make it new, vital

There is an imperfection
In these clumsy efforts
At faith, at love, at prayer
But sincerity leaves me unfettered

A hunger has emerged
A longing for more
Seeking, searching, listening
For His voice in the darkness

But this is no journey of doubt
More a quest born of hope
Steps toward completion
Of an interrupted formation

Voices, dead and living
Crowd my mind
Challenging, encouraging
These first movements through infancy

My brave new world
Lies beyond old assumptions
As faith and understanding begin anew
In His words which spring eternal

Your Best Work, Your Peak Years (01.29.17)

Now, at mid-life or beyond
You may be asking:
Is my best behind me?
The thrills of peak exertion
An apogee of capability
Lost forever in Time's grinding march
And perhaps gone with sinew
Are the golden aspirations
For worlds still unseen
Or the boundless energy
Of the incomplete self
Maybe passion's flame
Once burned brighter
Or newness hid behind every corner
You may ask: Where did it go?
As you consider things lost,
And the silent lamentations of age
Perhaps it's the mistakes and missteps
That feel more real
Or the "what could-have-beens"
That leave you longing
For that point when it was all before you

Walking with Conviction 2017-2020

Cast them aside!
These thoughts of loss and woe
The road is long, winding, and uncertain
For the mind that can ask
Still has a heart to answer
Take one more look at what was old
And in it you'll find something new
Those lines, those wrinkles
Mark distance traveled
But are no destination
The fleeting strength of youth
Defined but a moment
And then, in small ways
The hard-earned experience
Of grit and perseverance
Adds color and texture
To life's shifting frieze
Times and people,
Still unknown before gray hair and blemish,
Have formed you, shaped you
In wondrously unseen ways
Let go of doubt, fear, and regret!
For your peak years are happening now
And your best work is waiting to be realized

Traveler

That Moment (02.26.17)

The days walked past
As the tremor within intensified
Building moment to moment
In unseen tension
The kernel of doubt,
Once small and silly,
Magnified into a consuming blaze.
The burn was slow,
Until it wasn't.
Cascading forth
In a fierce rush of words, emotion
And the absolutes
Of fiery passion.
At that moment,
Life hangs at the edge
The vicissitudes multiply
Into a crescendo
Of "always" and "never"
Leaving no room
For the soft middle
Of empathy and understanding
That moment

Is an inflection point,
An emotional precipice
Where the heart of conflict
Might meet the bonds
Forged in other fires.
Hard words and fierce eyes
Mask the fragile self,
Stubborn, defiant, scared,
Hidden behind an iron mask
Of blame and pain.
That moment defines all,
For the ties left unbroken,
Become stronger,
While the lesser self
Retreats before the fraying justifications
Of self-righteousness and pride.

Traveler

Possibility (04.23.17)

That place of stillness
Suspended movement, arrested motion
Deep, sedentary thought
Almost detached
Within but aside
Even in the midst of an active world
It comes upon me
The sensation edges toward bliss
A serene pause
The confluence of possibility
Dreams from days and nights
Swirling, enveloping
No external indication
Of this kinetic moment
I see them all
Like pieces on a board
Primed for play
Dimensional, not linear
Forming, scattering
Seeing the moves ahead
Let me live here
Among possibility

Unencumbered by doubt
Or reality
Only the universe beyond
To hold this infinite array

In the Dark (04.29.17)

There is no escaping
The voices of doubt
Like endless drops of rain
Their incessant whispering
Echoes across the canyons of the mind
Piercing the soul
As so many dull arrows
No shortcuts or reprieve
They must be faced squarely
Faithfully
Mustering the deepest resolve,
Reserves of strength,
Pools of hope
Enjoined to careful protection
Of that most fragile self
In the dark
They are loudest
Most strong
In that insidious assault
On your foundation
Eroding each pillar
With a gnawing fear

Walking with Conviction 2017-2020

Until each calculation
Equates to unworthiness
And the last finger's grip
Begins to falter
Then He appears,
Walking across stormy waters
Calling you to
Be not afraid
And you know it shall pass
The dark, the storm, the drowning
All a passing test
Of a faith you haven't mastered
And a Grace you can never earn

When the Lights Go Out (05.04.17)

In the dark
You feel alone
Directionless
With no vision of the future,
But the black nothingness
Your mind wanders
To darker places
Further from hope
Or possibility
The voices whisper
Discouragement
And your limbs
Grow heavy with fear
Paralysis prevails
And with no point of reference
The hole grows wider, deeper
Drawing you to its bottomless,
Silent, despair
When the lights go out
Only doubt remains,
An all-consuming anxiety
Harboring the worst nightmares.

Walking with Conviction 2017-2020

Here, in the pit
Nothing but faith will prevail
Weakness will not carry you
But a sliver of trust might.
The faintest glimmer may penetrate
The black curtain of this night
Reminding you of the smallest gratitude.
The tiniest voice of possibility
May remind you of another place
Bright and warm, hopeful
When the lights go out
Your faltering strength
Must be directed
Toward a forgotten belief
In something more,
Something bigger,
Beyond the darkness
A place, a moment, a song
In which you rose beyond
The emptiness of doubt
To grasp the freedom of hope.
Silent it rests
There in the dark,
Patiently waiting for you

Traveler

Dreaming of Bernadette (06.03.17)

The prospect of our future
Moves me daily
With a constancy, reassuring and frightening
I imagine you kneeling
Before Our Lady
With your child's faith and curiosity
A vision familiar and strangely foreign,
I am struck by the serendipity
Timing and movements
Too curious to dismiss
As I consider your trust
In a vision, a feeling
You could not explain
Such is the nature of visions:
Inscrutable faith in uncertain futures
At least for those outside of them
Your steadiness inspires,
Affirms my own sense of direction
A purpose still not understood
All the while, the signs are there
Pointing toward a horizon
I'm just beginning to grasp

Walking with Conviction 2017-2020

You wait there, patiently
Innocent and unshakeable
Secure in a destiny
That was once unfathomable
As it is for us all

The Old Nemesis (06.09.17)

The clouds march slowly
Across the sky like an army of angels
White billowiness with gray severity
Moving toward the unknown
Beyond sight and sound

Tethered earthward by the world's hum
That unknown refuses to buttress fragility,
Withholding affirmation,
Leaving resented vulnerability
To wear as a cloak against joy.

The stillness passes
Onward, outward, away
Always away
A distant hammer, or bird
Calling the quiet into the unseen

Scores of similar moments
Flash across memory.
Days when there was nothing
But the impossible.
Nights when the fear
Eclipsed light from soul.

Walking with Conviction 2017-2020

All doors closed and the room contracted
Until each breath labored impotently
Against the hopelessness.
Here, that old nemesis, Doubt,
Stares back from the mirror
Launching each splinter of disappointment
As arrows against failing hope

Perhaps there is comfort
In his predictable appearance
The smooth edges of that offered crutch,
Given to rationalize weakness,
And a litany of excuses,
Explaining away the craven retreat of boldness

High atop the pine
A cardinal calls fearlessly,
Challenging the day,
With fiery plume and surety of flight
A steady defiance

"We are survivors," he cries
"Live this day
In its sunshine, breeze, and possibility.
Make your mark upon the world,
Deferring to nothing

Traveler

But your Creator,
And the beautiful purpose
For which He made you."

Cooper (06.24.17)

Suddenly, everything changed
My baby became a mother
She brought another human being
Into this world

The miracle was new again
In all of its emotional glory
The cry, unique to an infant
Ushering in this beginning

Seeing you takes me back
Birth is a singular moment
I see all of my children
Returning again in your birth

But that return is brief
For your arrival is different
You are your mom and your dad
Brought together uniquely

Your soft skin, smelling
As only babies do
Your hair, perfectly framing your head
Your eyes, blue and searching for our voices

Traveler

In you, I see the future
An era yet to be
Filled with possibility
Memories waiting to be made

It is all before you
And we buzz expectantly
With the discoveries you will make
The boy to be and the man beyond

I hope to be there with you
Loving, watching, being present
Giving you the best of me
In the way you need it

This is my prayer:
A faith-filled life for you
Wrapped in the love of family
Built on goodness, forged in adventure

With love I pen these first words
More are to be inspired
By you and your path ahead
May the road rise to meet you

Life of Opportunity (07.01.17)

In the tangled and messy
Chaos of existence
Lies the answer.
The calling to something more
Unordered and uncontrollable
A purpose worth having
Uncertain and wild
Pulling and pushing,
Our best self hides
Among the unseemly bramble
We call problems
Moving through and beyond
Requires tenacious will
In the pursuit of new answers
Paired with a willingness to listen
We must walk intentionally across the briar
And accept its afflictions,
For life waits along that path.
Experience dictates growth,
While growth reflects readiness
For the life we're meant to live
And the person we're called to be.

Sowing (07.15.17)

Prodigally
We cast ideas, efforts, and dreams
On the path, on the rock, among the thorns
Sometimes finding the fecundity of good soil

This seems a calling,
A firm persuasion to greater purpose
Reaching earthward,
Sowing for the fruits of possibility

To be all of which one is able
Is to plant liberally
Always reaping the results
Of deliberate aspiration.

Inscrutable Purpose (08.26.17)

The dew glistens on the grass
Reflecting the morning sun
In a glinting galaxy of blades
Fall's cool breath
Hinting at the seasons ahead
The change is coming
Turning another page
Sawgrass waves softly
In the morning breeze
While my heart wanders
Beyond sight
This moment is most difficult
Simply living it alone
A thousand distractions
Attempt to derail now
Hopes and fears
Equal culprits in sustaining restlessness
In the Now are birds and breeze
Stillness and contemplation
Seeking the quiet necessary
To hear His voice
No grand songs or loud calls

Traveler

Only a whisper, always a whisper
Like the steam from this coffee,
Ephemeral, passing
Visible for moments in the light
The glimpses are there
Soundbites along the way
If we stop to look and listen
So much noise allows us to hide.
In the silence, we seek the profound,
A lightning flash of clarity.
Alas, the bush does not burn,
The voice is far more subtle.
Life's directive whispered
One stone at a time
The danger is to cease trying
To submit without effort
It is through the grappling
That we discern the way.
Pushing self against the threshold
Sharpens intention and vision
Releasing control to purposeful allowance
We let this moment, and the next, happen
In a place where destiny refuses to bend.

I Choose Faith (09.14.17)

It is only now
That the future seems uncertain
Those moments ahead
Much more clear
Looking back

Today is always clear
Times and obstacles
Aligned before us
With unknown answers
And certain fears

Unspoken promises
And hard-earned faith
Grace holding hope
In the timeless embrace
Of uncertainty

In these days
We hold tightly the known,
Assumptions and beliefs
Forming our life raft
In rough waters

Traveler

Courage is the steel
Forged in fear
Our lonely ally
To vanquish doubt
And bolster resolve

These moments define us
Testing us against the rocks
Strengthening or breaking
As our spirit seeks firm ground
In the buffeting

The only answer, small steps
Backed by big faith
Innocent belief in good,
Faithful trust in beauty
Leading the way along the narrow paths

In this season
I choose the rough edges
Of the climb before
And the cuts and blisters
Strengthening my grip

I choose Faith
And its many splendors

Treasures to be discovered
In the voices reminding me
All will be ok

As You Leave (11.13.17)

My heart breaks
Oh, so slightly
As you leave
The day's gloom
Feels heavy on my soul
The light-filled moments before
Emptied unceremoniously
The sounds filling these empty rooms
Gone with the taillights
Turning the corner
The gift of time
Overwhelms me
As tears sharpen the edges
Of your departure
Had I forgotten my capacity to love?
The vulnerability of my affections
Has stripped my defenses
As I am laid bare
To these emotions
Gratitude remains
As emotion recedes
The steady pulse of a caring

That warms chilled bones
And chases shadows away
As you leave
The heartbreak lays quietly
Beside this most grateful love

Smiling, I Close My Eyes (01.07.18)

Though the surface has changed
The layers remain
Buried in timelessness
Anchoring me
No matter the progress
No matter
The demons of the night
Continue to call
Cloaked in stillness
These silent walls
Harbor the enemy
Ready to pounce
At the first sign of weakness
Though the devils
Are my own
I still try to hide,
To run away from my own creations
Always hoping for the miraculous
Always hoping
Smiling, I close my eyes
And remember
The distance is short

Walking with Conviction 2017-2020

But my memory is long
And gratitude rests also
In the shadows of empty rooms
My faith is not casual
And though the mistakes are mine
The way has been gloriously His.
This tale reads like impossible fiction
With serendipities too numerous,
Too perfect to be accidents
No, the moments reflect
The Divine in subtle mystery
My story suits a higher purpose
And I relinquish myself to it
The demons may come
But I know they'll pass
The challenges are real
But they are worthy
My heart is true
And though I am far from innocence
My love is pure
As I remain determined
To honor these gifts
Resolutely accepting
His generosity

Beacon (01.07.18)

A light for men
Calling each to more
An example worth following
Giving hope in possibility
A source of energy
Pushing and pulling equally
A standard
Worth measuring against
A reminder of the Divine
And the place for faith
In a world choosing its rejection
A source of comfort
During dark days
Let me be a beacon
Shining forth
Showing a way
Reminding others of their best parts
Waiting to be played
There is purpose in what we do
May we always remember it
May we always embrace it
No matter how dark our days

The Difference (01.07.18)

The difference lies
> In the little things

Quiet moments
> Away from the lights

Small movements
> Seemingly leading nowhere

The measure of our faith
> Mirrors what we give

The value of our existence
> Reflects the difference we make

Traveler

The Here and There of the Unseen (01.13.18)

I see You
In the white splendor
Morning's crisp call
To thoughts of the Divine

Freezing air touching my face
Roughly reminding me
Of man's fragile nature
The vulnerability of existence

In the frosty serenity
Lie a billion crystals
Hidden under the cold blanket
Whispering complexity

A sunrise reflection
Revealing what can be seen
While hinting at the invisible
His nature in, around, beyond

The stiff branches
Of pine and crabapple
Mark the horizon
In white pencil

Walking with Conviction 2017-2020

Tracing a randomness
But suggesting a pattern
A purpose unknowable
Mirroring a dimension beyond

We live in between
The known and the unknown
The dark and the light
Of Holy Mystery

Searching for traces
Connecting the dots
Of faith and reason
Trusting to His greater purpose

For that is Faith
Letting go while holding
Tightly to the rational
And the unfathomable

Today's wintry touch
Of silence and chill
Reminds me of the cold of the unknown
Held at bay by Faith's fire

Traveler

Her beauty and warmth
Reflected through windows
Separating and uniting
The here and there of the unseen

Twelve Months (02.10.18)

The distance, there to here
    Impossibly immense
        Passing so quickly

Changes wrought
    Along a journey
        You didn't realize had begun

Change is subtle
    In the moment
        Though distance multiplies

Tiny adjustments, persistently
    Altering space, time, heart
        Conforming the questing soul

The Divine Pointillist
    Painting the story of your life
        Even our brevity serves His purpose

The moments collect faster
    Revealing an image
        Only in rear view

It's best we can't connect the points

Traveler

Until distance gives perspective
    Else our hearts freeze in fear

The lines framing deep pools of experience
    Answer to that Painter
        Our face emerging anew

Looking back, I am surprised
    Affirmed in the joy
        Time writes across my brow

The distance still remarkable
    The surprises still unexpected
        The glory of it all clarified

While remnants of a hopeful optimism
    Reappear in the points
        Dotting these twelve months

Growing into You (02.15.18)

Outside the window
Day, night, rain, snow
Pass in their own mysterious way
Changing with time, in time
Marking all in a persistent reflection
Those seeds cast into the world
Grow, winding their way
Toward their own bright purpose
A destiny wrought through God's Plan
I am the joyful spectator
Watching all, sharing some
Of those defining moments
In their growing
Each winds and turns
Finding dead ends and side paths
To stretch in and around
Young, strong, and malleable
They bend in the winds
Even as their deep roots stabilize
It is a joy to experience
These lives lived
In their eyes is the sparkle

Traveler

A joie de vivre reflective
Of love and wonder
And I – I receive the gift
Of you, growing into you

Evening Sun (02.25.18)

You returned today
Bright-eyed
And warm
Illuminating pine and maple
With golden caresses
Chasing the gloom away
You brought hope and energy
Daffodils stretched toward you,
Happily
The melancholy chill dissipated
And we all turned westward
To embrace your brief visit
In your light, all things show more lovely
Winter's hazy trail across windowpanes,
A bit less dingy in your glowing return
For my part, I'll give thanks to your Creator
Our Divine Author willing you upon us
Affirming our place in His Grace
While we place ourselves
Directly in your soul-warming embrace

Scars (03.05.18)

Show me your scar
And I'll show you mine
The low line of jagged edges
Pink, tender, raw
Hiding pains
Still carried

Tell me your story
And I'll tell you mine
Hurt and triumph
Suffering that seemed endless
Until it wasn't
Dark nights giving way to bright dawns

Show me your hope
And I'll show you mine
Unearned salvation
And faith in the Divine
Supra-rational thinking
Bringing me to embrace the mysteries

Release your pain
And I'll release mine
Together we agree,

Hurt no longer our master
Only a willing guide
To the better side of ourselves

Falling Days (05.11.18)

The mindless
    frenetic energy
        of stress

Consuming, gripping
    no closure – only the deep fall
        moving, racing

Never complete, never full
    rapacious is the gnawing
        clawing emptiness

Pulling back is difficult
    feeling and emotion
        refusing to let go

There is no escape
    solo effort inadequate
        a deeper faith required

Eyes closing, heart slowing
    surrendering something
        that never really mattered

Reaching for a truth
    a love that beckoned
        all along

The Choice (06.06.18)

There is no faith without doubt
No courage without fear
No way forward without obstacles
These are the trials
The way of man
There can be no gain without loss
No love without hate
We cannot recognize light without dark
Here we find ourselves stumbling
Before we can run again
The edge defines us
On it we must balance
To fall over either side
Is to lose perspective –
And self
We cannot retreat
Without losing something within
Forward we are called
Tiptoeing across oblivion
We are formed
In the stretch between moments
Forged solid and straight

Or warped and unsteady
Ahead is the way
The time for the choice has come
Meaning nothing less,
Than everything

The Truth (06.10.18)

The way it is
Reality
Not impression, perception, or interpretation
Truth
We seek it
Want it
But seldom recognize it
Our truth
His truth
The truth
Why is water wet?
And what is wetness?
We know it to be
It is a fact
But the truth of it is obscure
This world of twisting, turning
Pseudo-reality
Persists in hiding the truth
Behind motivations and obfuscations
Intent, word, and action
We intend the truth
Or we don't

Walking with Conviction 2017-2020

We speak the truth
Or we don't
We live the truth
Or we don't
Perhaps we never knew the truth

Shreds (06.12.18)

As if hoping
Would change anything
The cold, brittle reality
Etched in days
Moody and gray
Optimism fades
Under pressure,
Such crushing weight
The schemer's machinations
Empty and ephemeral
Once promising
Then gone
The wisp of possibility
Still hanging in the air
Unpleasant and certain
As the thorn's prick
Resisting the way forward
That inner voice
Quiet now
As the night begins
His howls of impotence
Sent from the dark place

Where all light goes out
Leaving only
The shreds of our belief

Reunion (06.12.18)

Across the lot,
I saw you emerge
Eyes wandering blankly
Dimmed by broken sleep
And travel's hypnosis
Mom, bright and energetic,
Scooping you up,
Nearly bounding to the door
Your small shape barely visible
Against mom's outline
Baby and boy
And energy coiled to spring
You surveyed the strange bustle
Of cars, people, sounds
Removed from it
While suspended within it
Moving toward you
I caught your eye
Ah, the familiar!
A faint smile emerged
As our eyes locked
And you tracked me,

Five, four, three, two,
Steps to you
And the world stopped
Silent, without hesitation
You reached for me
And the world came to life

Why? (07.10.18)

The morning dove
Calls to the day
Is it a sound of sadness?
Or a whisper of hope?
The trees are silent
Like so many loved ones
Here but gone
Their light graced us
For a moment,
Now we ask, why?

The day's challenges await
Grinding, turning, crushing
We live within life's mill
Hulled and husked
Broken along the way
There is no call
No song for our toils
Unseen, we push forward
Toward an unknown end
Asking all the while, why?

Today, I pick up the banner

Walking with Conviction 2017-2020

Armed and armored
Moving to the horizon
Summoning those who would rally
Toward distant objectives
They follow, blindly
Steeled with my certainty
They charge forward
Trusting in the mysteries
Of my imagination, why?

In this valley of tears
There is hunger and pain
Seeking the salve of hope
Calling in the dark
For direction, for guidance
For one hand to hold
And the Lamb's voice
To whisper: it's all ok
Follow me
I'll show you why

I Walk On (07.15.18)

The test is time
Pressure applied over distance
Endurance demanded
But reluctant
Pushing through,
The most excruciating exercise
Of mind, spirit, sinew
Retreat, a constant echo
Of the fear ever present
Make it stop
Please God
Not mine
But Your Will be done
Unforsaken
Undeserving
Unrelenting
I walk on
Always on

Faith (08.02.18)

At once solid
Rocklike in steady strength
Certain as the sky
Armored for travail
Then fleeting
Wispy and wind-like
Shifting with life's breeze
Running before life's trials
We long for the steady comfort
Of a faith made immovable
For the strength of conviction
And its defense against doubt
But our faith stands
On human frailty
Bends with mortal fear
Retreats from our own weakness
We are not made to stand alone
Only His hand might steady us
We are reeds in the wind
Only roots in His soil
Hold us in place

Each Step (08.03.18)

My heart beats full
Overflowing with all
That I cannot hold within
My cross looks light
Next to true troubles
The brokenhearted, the defeated
The broken
But in the smallest soul
I find the most
Hope and happiness
A light burning brightly
Innocent and joyful
The steps come slowly
The barriers are many
But that tiny heart
Beats fiercely
Holding to life intensely
Not questioning or doubting
But living, just living
Each and every faltering step

Walking with Conviction 2017-2020

The Evening Calls (08.24.18)

The evening calls
Moody and cool
Replete with the sounds of life
Harboring secrets in the folds
Of its descending cloak
The night's music echoes
Hauntingly beckoning,
Calling us to some other experience
At once sad and hopeful
The song announces change
The day, the week, the season
The bulldog is restless
Her permanent scowl twitching
With the shifting breeze
Sensing the impending shift
From long days and warm air
Those of us on two legs
Fret about chasing the night's promises
And tomorrow's possibilities
Oblivious to the shifting sands
Moving beneath our feet
Impervious to lost moments

Traveler
___

Scattered across our distractions
The world moves on
And we wait for a sign

Remembering (09.03.18)

Cooper's eyes pass
Over photos of moments past
Bright days reflected
In his shiny orbs
Point to the images,
He seems to ask "Who is that?"
And I smile as I say Grandpa Great Roy
Looking deeper, I return
To those times, those places
Not realizing how fleeting they were
We smiled, alive and together.
Across the room
The heron reminds me
Of our new reality
No longer new
Our world has changed
And Cooper will only know how
By the stories we tell
We live as if
The days will last forever
Forgetting that we won't
Looking closely,

Traveler

I see Sally in your eyes
A photo remembers well
And I have to laugh to myself
Because it was happy
And we're better
For having known you
And though our grandchildren
Will never know your humor
Or laugh
We'll tell the stories
Giving wing to your spirit
And substance to your photos
Making them real again
For all of us

News (09.24.18)

Soft rain and gray
Mark the morning
The light breeze
Intermittently chills and refreshes
The buzz of the morning rush
Fills the air
Present but indistinct

Fall sneaks in
Stealthy
Like family at midnight
Promising change
While green leaves resist
The season starts to turn
Toward that waiting horizon

You called me
Video image of angelic joy
Giddy with news
Unable to contain
Word of the light within
Your own season shifting
Toward that life now present

Traveler

The news seems unreal
Even as its magnitude
Slowly permeates this reality
Hinting at a future
New and unknown
With all of the fears, joys, and possibilities
That new life brings

I see God in such news
Feel the Holy Spirit
Present amid the joy
Your openness to life
Reflects the Divine
Showing a faith, a love
Bringing me pride beyond measure

As heavenly waters
Feed new life
This day mirrors the nourishing effects
Of love and faith
For your unborn
One and separate with you

We will wait patiently
Walking with you as we can
Joining your joy

Walking with Conviction 2017-2020

Loving your love
Holding fast to faith
And it's great possibility
Changing with this new season

Changes (11.03.18)

The sounds of life
Fill this house
Voices bring fullness
To its empty spaces
Laughter echoes
Across waiting walls

It's so easy to forget
The times past
Moments in the building years
Uncountable
Then gone too quickly
Yielding to life's waning

We take much for granted
Chasing dreams among days
We thought would last
Life's grand parade
Carrying us along
Imperceptibly

These days
A new waxing appears
Rich and textured

Walking with Conviction 2017-2020

In ways forgotten
New stories and voices
Marking time in fresh strokes

The melancholy
Of the lost
Weighs heavily
But breaks before
The new lightness,
A renewed hope in this day's dawn

Gratitude bears all
Amid the joy of these discoveries
And the hustle and bustle
Of racing forward
Retreats to steadiness;
Life's new pace happily embraced

Gratitude (11.22.18)

Our blessings
Reflect the Divine
In our lives

Our gratitude
Echoes hope
In His promise

Our sharing
Manifests these gifts
In loving action

January Spring (01.08.19)

Rain and warmth
Blankets this morning
In hopeful melancholy
The longing for another time
Layered on expectant waiting
Leaving Now inert and alone
We live our lives
In this in-between,
Caught between lost moments
And better days ahead
This January Spring
Conspires to deceive us
The gray clouds
Warm and suggestive
Of a season whose time has not yet come

Enough (01.28.19)

You are,
Enough

The cold, icy wind
Bearing down, pushing, threatening,
Freezing that part of you
Fighting for tomorrow
Displacing today's hope
With the doubt of night
Inside, you rail, you scream
But the only sound is a whisper

You are,
Enough

The gales rush against you
As the way narrows
Your limbs stiffen
Your feet grow heavy
Your heart falters
And your vision dims
Dark resistance,
Then faltering

Walking with Conviction 2017-2020

You are,
Enough

Light, briefly appears
The slow glow of tomorrow
Breaking across the bleakness
Fear grips you, but the kernel of belief emerges,
Hope returns
And your retreat evokes rage,
Fierce anger, focused
Piercing the doubt with fiery intent

You are,
Enough

Breaking free,
You shake the night's icy grip
With a glance toward possibility
Running now
The airy lightness returns
As you leap, hopeful
Soaring past fear's calumny
Retreating below

You are,
Enough

The Book of Eli (05.12.19)

Haunting
Are those sounds
Music that takes me away
A story. A journey. A discovery.
What we thought we were protecting
Was within us all along
Such is our journey of faith
Grace and forgiveness
Have been given
We just need to accept
And allow our selves
To fall closer to Him
Eli trusted
In something he could not see
So we are called.
Haunting
Those sounds take me there
And beyond

Intersection (05.12.19)

This convergence
Weighs lightly on me
Striking a balance of directions
Moving in, more than away
I see life's threads crossing
All that was
All that will be
Suspended here, I pause
At this intersection
Seeing it all clearly
Feeling acutely
The love. The loss.
The struggle. The victory.
Threads in the same fabric
Joy rests there – solid and fleeting
To be held. To be released.
To be rediscovered.
These are the patterns of existence
This is the intersection

Reflection (06.30.19)

The screen is dark
With no bits or bytes
No flashing color or image
Holding only my outline

No lines or wrinkles
Mark that countenance
Even thin, wispy hairs seem full
Faceless and youthful

We are all outlines
Shells waiting
For the world
To be poured within

But the shadow reflection
Shows little of the energy within
Synapses firing between those ears
A world alive beneath

We so oft live like that
All outline with shadowed detail
Giving little of what lies beyond
Sharing naught of those electric thoughts

Walking with Conviction 2017-2020

Today, I'll take those shadows
And contemplate their place
The forms full and complex
In a light cast from beyond

For we are but feathery reflections
Of the Divine moving us
All possibility and little clarity
Darkened in our unlit formation

Reagan (06.30.19)

You came into the world
With a kick and a cry
Received in the love
Of those who have waited
Your skin, baby soft
Touched by air for the first time
And your eyes, deep, gray darkness
Struggling to follow those voices calling
Long, slender, fingers grasping
Seeking mommy and her touch
Moments before, just a dream
Your voice, innocent and pleading
Knowing only comfort or discomfort
Seeking the sounds to summon
We crowded into your room
Smiling widely until
Our jaws hurt
Our own voices seeking yours
Welcoming and loving you
The words fall short of the moment
Images now fading
Fail to capture the warmth

Even your brother,
Confused and disoriented as you
Recognized the moment as special
And transformative
Now begins the long journey
Toward life, experience, God
We will walk with you as we can
Always loving, always knowing,
Always being what we can for you
Remembering these beginnings,
We hold you close
And gaze into your searching eyes
Hopeful and affectionate
Seeing it all before you

Dawn (08.06.19)

Beyond the trees
Full and green and strong
The restless clouds loom
Reflecting the edge
Of a horizon I can't quite see

The colors gray blue, pale pink
Frame and otherworldly wisdom
Timeless and penetrating
At once here and beyond
Beckoning and aloof

Such is the world's indifference
Enfolding us as it casts us out
Promising more
While letting us stumble
In the acceptance of less

I see the shapes of the Divine
Cast across the world about me
And ponder their mystery
Longing for the peaceful promise
While reveling in the struggle

Walking with Conviction 2017-2020

The days seem long
But they grow short
While we chase the phantoms
Of some life unlived
Just beyond our imagination

One dead tree mars
The vision
Reminding me of the fading light
That accompanies each dawn
Inevitably darkening its destiny

The colors shift with time
And I see the present clearly
Pressing with its urgencies
Even while I float a bit longer
Holding as best I can

The Things We Found (11.11.19)

In the mountains, we found an edge
A place where our bodies stopped
Pushed to the limits
Then the strength to push on

In the villages, we found history
Time and story beyond imagination
Great deeds and sad tales
Then the hope to move forward

On the road, we found others
Searching for something
Beyond the known
Then the inspiration to take another step

In the cathedrals, we found beauty
Rising to the heavens
inspired by God
Then the faith to trust

In the cities, we found frenzy
The maelstrom of life
Unfettered by our purposes
Then the energy to keep going

Walking with Conviction 2017-2020

In the wind, we found fear
The doubt of our own reasons
Pushing against our progress
Then the courage to walk anyway

In the rain, we found despair
An oppressive resistance
Whispering "Why are you doing this?"
Then the will to believe

In each other, we found purpose
Bound by something higher
Calling us to more
Then the promise of brighter days

In You, we found faith
The unreasonable belief
In our own worth
Then the Trust to follow You to the end

Santiago (11.12.19)

The rain held us
In its cold cocoon
Blanketing us
While the tornado
Swelled within
Arrival was bittersweet,
Frenetic at first
Settling to placid introspection
All emotion seemed magnified
Each feeling epic
Searching for meaning,
We strained our senses
Reaching for firm ground
Hoping for revelation
Stories swirled between us
Memories even now fading
As the suffering evaporated
And the salt of different earth remained
Under the spires
We held tightly to our trials

Within the sepulcher
We wondered at the mystery

Walking with Conviction 2017-2020

Even now, unsure
Your wet, stone streets
Offered no answers
Only the echo of rain drops
The flow of pilgrims
Marked the moments
Running like blood,
Then washing away
We found it here
Walking into your arms
Where the waiting smiles
And affection greeted us
The simple humanity of the moment
Answered many questions
There is much left unsaid
But we leave you, knowing love
Our next steps resting on something solid
Something that wasn't there before

Pilgrim (11.12.19)

Words are often meaningless,
Until we grow into them
There are no shortcuts
To that person we might become
We must be forged
On the roads we travel
Choosing our Way,
We walk forth
Carrying so much
Finding we need less
Than we ever imagined
Our path is marked
By the detritus left behind
Our hope is found
In hidden places along the Way
You started this journey
Claiming the Word
Praying you had strength enough
To meet its demands
But there was no way to know
Those trials you would face
No way to know the price you would pay

Walking with Conviction 2017-2020

To move forward on faith alone
Requires courage
But your faith was in yourself
And not enough for the Way ahead
Those first bold steps
Led to the faltering ones to follow
You had to break
Before wholeness could be found
There is a lifetime hidden on this Way
Finding it, demands all of you
Hills and valleys
Sun and rain
Wind and tears
The road took all
And gifted it back
We walk through our lives
Blinded by the bright, the shiny
Here, you found the dull and the worn
Time and distance made it
Just for you
Here, you realized that your faith was not enough
The Way called you to more
The You that existed before
Must yield to the one to be born
The faith you held before

Traveler

Must be broken to be remade
In the old, you found new
And the many hands reaching for you
Held you through the rain
Cleansing you through baptism
Of a different kind
You set forth unsure of what you might find
Arriving, they called you Pilgrim
Arriving, you found all that you left behind

Finisterre (11.13.19)

Infinito,
The word hung in brass
With the endlessness of the Atlantic
Framing it beyond

The end of the world
Feels poised at the edge
Of infinity
A step from oblivion

O Semaforo
Was a fitting end
To the days and nights of trial
A form of completion to the Way

The dark waters worked tirelessly
Shaping the edges of a world
Resistant to change
Sculpting it to its place among us

Here, at the end
Our hearts and minds wandered
Back to St. Jean where we started
And across the dark waters to what's next

Traveler

Our journey continues to illuminate us
As the light slowly brings clarity to this day
Like the tiny boats below,
We float and bob to the rhythm of its deep waters

That rhythm still calls to us
Pilgrims now of a different sort
The life that was, yields to what must be
We, forever changed in its forming

Finisterre welcomed us,
And will soon return us
To that new rhythm –
The life after the journey

Here at the edge of the world
It all seems possible
The baptism of the Way
Releasing us to new life

The Way (11.23.19)

For years you dreamed it
The adventure of a lifetime
Promising possibility
Unlikely, even impossible
It floated there
A constant point in the universe
Under which you moved,
Walking the path of the routine
You spoke of it, wrote of it
Always there, waiting
Somewhere in the future
Too far to be real
The days passed
And the dream remained
Until that distant point
Appeared closer
Now visible among your stars,
Lining up at the end
Of a long runway, skyward
Here, you started running
Building speed to take flight
For so long it beckoned you remotely,

Traveler

Now it was real and approaching
The blurring moments
Moved you along until the time had come
And you found yourself there,
No longer dreaming
Now in it, now walking it
Crossing that threshold where your world ended,
Life slowed to a crawl
And all you expected exploded,
Scattered across a different reality
And you realized you were no longer dreaming
But that too moved along, quickly
The slow holding slipped from your fingers
And moved heavenward
Even while you fell to the earth
Firm ground again
With nothing but the whisper
Of a dream that once was
And then distance placed it
In that constellation of your life
Called memory
As your eyes turned toward the next horizon
And the sunrise of the day you forgot to expect.

The Next Step (01.09.20)

The next step,
Is the hardest.
The next breath,
The sharpest.
The next moment,
The loneliest.
The next day,
The emptiest.

How do I cross the distance?
The miles between here
And the return of joy
Seem incalculable
There is no comfort
There are no answers
Only the next step.

Walking Away (02.13.20)

You turned
And walked away
The door slammed
In complete finality
For a moment
It all hung in the air
Then fell into emptiness
My heart stirred
Shaken with a sense of loss
The closing of something else
The drama held me
Then moved on as well
Such is the way of moments
Lost in the crush of time
And surrender
Looking at the pen beckoning
I held my breath,
Then let it all go.
One exhale, one choice
The pen called.
Forward motion

Walking with Conviction 2017-2020

Steady (03.24.20)

The sand shifts under foot
Waves pushing and pulling
Removing steadiness
In their retreat
These are days of unease
Unsteadiness
A time when certainty
Feels distant,
A stranger to our longing.
The vulnerability has returned
Though it was never far
All the old rules feel broken
The old comforts, a mirage
In this blanket of doubt,
We reach, casting about
For one hand

To make us steady

Searching for one voice
In our concrete wilderness
Even the slightest whisper will do
Instead, we find a cacophony

Traveler

The agitation of the masses
Seething with anxiety
Desperate with doubt
Behind that gray curtain
Hides the lightest touch
A fluttering breeze
Soft and steady.
Promising firm footing
In that shifting sand
Grasping, grasping
We stretch toward it
But too late
It already found us
Fragrant, warm, soothing

Steady

The whisper comes, finally
It sounds like hope
Certain, firm

Steady

One *for Reagan* (05.23.20)

What is one?

One is your smile
And your moving feet
The steps you take,
The eyes you meet

One is a special party
Thrown to celebrate
Gathered all for you
Singing loud, staying late

One is your laugh
The giggling of innocence
The time we shared
And Beau, running 'round the fence

One is today, this moment
We all showed up for you
Holding you close
Giving love too

Traveler

Toward a Waiting Tomorrow (11.25.20)

The day passes
Toward a waiting tomorrow
Framed in the rain's cool embrace
Hiding pending uncertainty.
The desirable displaced
By the unknowable
But hope lives on
Resting in the arms
Of a hard-won faith
Such times demand
Mettle of a different sort
The resolve of will
Forged of something more
Cast to hold
Yet molded to bend
The weight of all
Straining those foundations
I care not for doubt
And the dramas of men
It is a Divine tune
To which I dance

And these girders
Hold while others falter.
Defiant in malleable surrender

JMJ for Fulton (03.28.21)

Blessed is your namesake,
Upon whose footprints
Did we set your tiny feet
Knowing that you too
Would be called to sainthood.
For that is *our* calling
Each set upon the path,
Of God's Perfect Plan

Strong is your name
You did not disappoint
Healthy and robust
Like Mom, like Dad
But there is more,
Already more
As your smile emerges
Equally so your growing spirit

Can we pin hopes
On a babe? Do we dare?
Each precious soul,
One more chance
To change the world

One more chance
To bring hope
One more chance.

O little one,
You too are called
His name written
Across your heart.
Your strength grows
In days passing
Each marked with faith,
Each sustained with love

Our prayer for you remains,
That you know His Goodness
As you follow the wisdom
Of those come before,
That you feel His Grace
Along the ways of your life,
That you live freely, hopefully,
Knowing you are cherished

Traveler (04.12.21)

Beginning, that long horizon
Seemed endless
The time ahead, interminable
But the distances
Were never so far
And time passed quickly

Dreams lay always out there
Somewhere ahead
But the striving
Often turned to grasping
And the day's moments
Surrendered to tomorrow's desires

Pursuing destinations,
The journey seemed all arrivals
Ends consuming the means
Today, never enough
The Traveler's restlessness
Looking forever ahead

Sometimes pilgrim,
But often tourist,
The days alternated

Walking with Conviction 2017-2020

Between actively seeking
and passively watching
While all flowed past

Along the way,
Signs began to appear
Pointing at first toward the small
Then toward more,
Of a different sort
So often lost amid the fleeting moments

The pause and the breath,
Deep inhalation of the now
Prompting reflection
Demanding another look
At the approaching horizon
Now oriented to something else

Those destinations once so clear,
Now hazy with experience
The needs, wants, hopes
Blurred by necessity,
Recast with fresh eyes
And awakened soul

Unexpected hunger,

Traveler

Changed the trajectory
An unseen path emerged
Calling with siren song,
Revealing secrets
Once invisible

Alerted to the signals
The Traveler awakes
To the path now cast
In brighter light,
The horizon closer still
And the road rising purposefully

About the Author

Entrepreneur. Author. Leader. Poet. Phillip Berry is Founder and CEO of Northwind Pharmaceuticals, based in Indianapolis, Indiana. His first book, Stones Across the River, was published in 2016 and focuses on doing your best  work in your peak years. His second book, Every Day is Game Day, published in 2018, calls readers to show up every day ready to be the best version of themselves. From creating new businesses and renovating old buildings to coaching, parenting, grandparenting, and serving, Phillip works to marry his Catholic faith with a sense of mission for the communities and people in his life.

www.ingramcontent.com/pod-product-compliance
Lightning Source LLC
Chambersburg PA
CBHW030431010526
44118CB00011B/585